Bill Barnes
8/18/97

Memories of God

Memories of God

THEOLOGICAL REFLECTIONS ON A LIFE

Roberta C. Bondi

ABINGDON PRESS
Nashville

MEMORIES OF GOD
THEOLOGICAL REFLECTIONS ON A LIFE

Copyright © 1995 by Abingdon Press

This book is printed on recycled, acid-free paper.

Library of Congress Cataloging-in-Publication Data

Bondi, Roberta C.
    Memories of God : theological reflections on a life / Roberta C.
Bondi.
        p.   cm.
    ISBN 0-687-03892-8 (alk. paper)
    1. Bondi, Roberta C.   2. Theologians—United States—Biography.
3. Theology, Doctrinal.   4. Prayer—Christianity.   5. Women in Christianity.   I. Title.
BX4827.B56A3   1994
230'.033'092—dc20   94-37755
[B]   CIP

Scripture quotations noted NRSV are from the New Revised Standard
Version Bible, copyright © 1989 by the Division of Christian Education of
the National Council of the Churches of Christ in the USA. Used by
permission.

Illustrations by John Boegel

96 97 98 99 00 01 02 03—10 9 8 7 6 5 4 3

MANUFACTURED IN THE UNITED STATES OF AMERICA

◊ CONTENTS ◊

◊ INTRODUCTION ◊

The following book is a collection of stories. When I was a child I loved stories. A timid little girl who was afraid of everything, I loved the stories of the brave Madeleine: "She was not afraid of mice; she loved winter, snow and ice. To the tiger in the zoo, Madeleine just said 'pooh, pooh.'" A lonely child who could never seem to fit in, I loved fairy tales like Beauty and the Beast and the Ugly Duckling. A child who worried about God and the cosmic meanings of things, I loved stories from the Old Testament. I particularly favored ones featuring children: Joseph and his brothers, Isaac and Abraham, and Ruth, whom I always pictured not as an adult woman but as a little girl like me.

For me, as for almost all children, I suspect, stories were not just entertainment; they were my lifeblood. They helped me make sense of myself, my family, and my world. True, they sometimes gave me explanations of who I should be and why I was unhappy that were destructive to me as a female child. They also, however, offered me new ways of seeing and thinking about things that stretched me far beyond my childhood unhappiness to envision other ways of being, other worlds. The Madeleine stories did this for me, reared as I was according to the model of the perfect, pliant, ladylike little girl. So did the story of Joseph, who was hated by his brothers for his interpretation of dreams, thrown into a pit, and sold into slavery in Egypt, where he finally was made ruler.

During my high school and college years I continued to love stories for the same reasons. Dostoevski's *Crime and Punishment* and *The Brothers Karamazov,* Camus's *Plague,* and Thomas Hardy's *Tess of the d'Urbervilles* were among my favorites. They talked explicitly about God, and the significance and goal of human lives, and in that unhappy and confused period of my life I had a voracious appetite for these subjects. In significant ways, I believe now, these novels, along with most others that I read, hurt me as they reinforced the stereotypes of women I was already receiving from my larger culture of the late fifties and early sixties. Nevertheless, it was thinking about all these things through the lenses of the adult stories I encountered that equipped me to tell myself my own story, to question, to imagine, to interpret in new ways my life and the world in which I lived. It wasn't comfortable a lot of the time, and it even got me in trouble, but it was worth it. Though at the time I wouldn't have articulated it to myself in these terms, I knew that this was what theology was about.

When I got to seminary, however, I encountered something else. In the sixties liberalism of theological education there was a hierarchy of truth. There, theology was an esoteric discipline that did not like stories, even biblical stories, unless they were of the sort like *The Old Man and the Sea* and *Waiting for Godot* that could be stripped free of their particulars in order to get at the universal meaning of their symbolism. This was because serious theology concerned itself only with what theologians assumed was universally true. It did not waste its time addressing the personal and the "subjective," the everyday or the particular. Certainly, there was no room in theology to raise any of the kinds of questions I had, especially those connected with my own experience as a female human being. Theology was abstract, logical, propositional, and systematic, and so was its God.

This hurt. Still, since I wanted to be a serious person and do serious work, during the years of my graduate work at Oxford I tried to exchange my habit of thinking about my own life through the medium of stories for "objective" thinking. I did my best to hold my "objective" self separate from my pressing questions about what the material I was studying had to say to me as a woman. I became a historian of Christian thought, and I was successful enough at it that I was able to write a good dissertation on the most abstract and central of all patristic theological topics, the christological controversies of the fifth century.[1]

It was during the same graduate years, however, that I also discovered in the writings of the early church the ancient, not so "serious" monastic tradition. The monastic teachers of the first generations of monasticism approached the great questions of human life and the way God relates to us not through abstract theological statements but through the medium of sayings and stories that take the world of individual experience very seriously. This discovery of a congenial way of doing theology in the early tradition was wonderful for me. Though at that time there was no respectable way to talk about this theological tradition in academic circles back home, it was this early monastic way of thought that really aided me in beginning to think through some of the painful questions that gripped me.

Once I started teaching, however, I felt obligated to teach the history of early Christian thought in the same

1. Published under the name Roberta C. Chesnut as *Three Monophysite Christologies: Severus of Antioch, Philoxenus of Mabbug, and Jacob of Sarug* (New York: Oxford University Press, 1976).

mode as I had been taught it by my own teachers. At the same time I was only too aware that by making this choice I was perpetuating in my students the same problems I had had in my own education. I was stifling their most pressing questions and encouraging them to believe that reflection on their own experience in light of the theology they were studying was only a private, pious exercise. Yet even in my seminary and graduate years I always knew that what should make theology valuable was precisely what was being rejected as not-theology.

Theology, I would now say, is about saving lives, and the work of theology, to use Rebecca Chopp's phrase,[2] is saving work. First, it involves learning to see the ways in which false images of God, ourselves, and the world have bound us and taken away the life God intends for us. Second, it involves learning to know God as God is, as a healing God, and learning to know ourselves, individually and communally, as people who correspond with that God in whose image we are made. Third, it involves imagining a future that is consistent with the God we come to know.

We can do this saving work, I believe, however, only as our imagination is captured, and we are able at the deepest level to take our own experience, our own lives

---

2. See *Saving Work: Feminist Practices of Theological Education* (Louisville: Westminster/John Knox Press, 1994).

seriously. For this reason, I began to teach more and more of the literature of the early church that made use of stories, sayings, and saints' lives to talk about the real human experience that theology is supposed to address, and I increasingly encouraged my students in the classroom to find ways to bring their own experience and theological convictions into conversation with the ancient material.[3]

While this new way of teaching was evolving, I also began a daily discipline of prayer that committed me to facing many issues that had hurt me for a long time. The method of this prayer involved a careful and painful examination of my life and of my corresponding theology as it had affected me since childhood. As part of the process, I often found myself recounting to myself stories of my own life in the presence of God. From the beginning I found the telling of these stories amazingly helpful in all sorts of ways. I gained embarrassing but freeing insights into what I actually believed in my heart about God, the world, myself, and other people—as opposed to what I had thought I believed, but didn't. I learned fairly early on, for example, that whatever I had

---

3. This is the approach I have used in my two books on the spirituality of the early monastic tradition as a resource for modern Christians: *To Love as God Loves: Conversations with the Early Church* (Minneapolis: Augsburg-Fortress, 1987) and *To Pray and to Love: Conversations on Prayer with the Early Church* (Augsburg-Fortress, 1991).

wanted to believe about God as loving, what I really believed was that God's favorite activity was criticizing and condemning.

Also becoming clear to me through the telling of my stories in my prayer was how often what I had regarded as my own personal, private hurts were really not so private or idiosyncratic when they were seen in the context of the intersection of my theological beliefs, my family experience, and the larger world of modern and ancient cultural expectations into which my theology and my personal experience fit. This was particularly true with a whole range of difficulties I had around the issue of being female, but it was true with many other issues for me as well.

Once all this began to become clearer, I found myself able to begin to re-envision at the intellectual level other actual theological possibilities, another future for my own life, as well as for the life of the church and of human society itself. But how to move from theoretical possibilities to knowing them as true in your very bones? Luke reports Jesus to have told his disciples "ask, and it will be given you; search, and you will find; knock, and the door will be opened for you."[4] For me, it was only as I was able to tell these stories of my own life to God that I was even able to hear for myself what

---

4. Luke 11:9 NRSV.

it was I needed to ask God for, to ask for it, and to receive it.

Nevertheless, having been well trained by my education not to talk in scholarly circles about anything so private and personal as my own life, much less about prayer, I would not even have dreamed of writing about what I was learning about any of this until a few years ago, when I began to attend a series of summer consultations at the Institute for Ecumenical and Cultural Research in Collegeville, Minnesota. These consultations were conducted in such a way that for a week each summer the various participants would gather to discuss a single theological theme, such as incarnation or the content of Christian hope. Though the themes differed from year to year, every summer the consultations began the same way: during the first two days each of us was asked to reflect on the theological topic under discussion, not as good representatives of the traditions we came from but through the lens of our own experience.

The process of telling and listening to these stories was hard work. Though I had begun in my prayer to know the significance of telling God and myself stories of my life, I had never been asked to talk publicly about the meaning of a particular Christian doctrine specifically in this way, nor had I had the chance to listen to other people's stories. It took thinking about what we had believed in the past and in the present as well as what the history of Christian thought had had to say on the topic. It demanded a serious consideration of what in our lives had brought us to believe as we did, and how our convictions had been helpful or hurtful to us as children, as adults, as women and men, as members of our Christian communities, and as citizens.

For myself, I found this approach to theology incredibly profitable. To begin, there was the matter of wonder and gratitude. In organizing the "facts" of my life I was asked for, I was struck in a way I never had been before by a kind of awe and gratitude to God for the gift of my own particular life, of the very life I had led. Never before, I think, had I actually been glad that I was me and not somebody else. This was half the gift. The other half came as I listened to other people reflecting theologically on their own very diverse experiences. Just to hear their stories filled me in a new way with a holy wonder and gratitude both for the reality of each separate human life and the mystery of God's presence in it.

Second, there was the matter of the universal and the individual, the public and the private. It was only in bringing myself to talk in front of the other consultation members about what I had been trained to regard as academically and socially taboo that I really could see for myself how deep and how wrong is the split we assume we must make between the publicly acceptable and the private in our churches and in academics. As individuals this split between public and private silences us on the very things that matter to us most. It makes us unable to fight for ourselves, or even to imagine new ways of thinking, feeling, and relating. It makes our churches, our families, and our friendships boring and sometimes even deadly. It causes us to compartmentalize or try to discard parts of ourselves that don't fit with the publicly acceptable.

This split makes us forget that our private, experiencing "selves," even our Christian selves, do not come unmediated from our own insides or even from God. Rather, we are formed in very complex ways by our social experiences of family, church, school, and friends, by our larger culture and its expectations, as well as by scripture, and by the Christian tradition. Failing to recognize the communal origins of our "private" selves makes us identify points of pain in ourselves as "personal problems," and as a result we are not able to see how often the "personal" is, in fact, intimately linked with the social and cultural. This observation, of course, has been one of the great insights of the women's movement in the last few decades.

But how can we ever be healed theologically, individually, unless we refuse to accept a split in our own selves between what is publicly and what is privately acceptable—until we can find a way to tell our own stories, hear one another's stories, and learn to tell them again in new ways? Until we can talk about our prayer and our theological convictions and our life experiences as all part of the same piece? At Collegeville, I finally accepted that the theological work of telling one another our stories, of talking about the ways in which our concrete and particular experiences intersected with the great Christian doctrines was not private work, or work done only on behalf of each of us as individuals. It was a common work, real theology done in order to find a way to claim for our own time and our own generation what it means to be Christian.

Gradually, as I prayed, taught, and thought about all of this I began to conceive of a theological project in which, by means of reflecting on my own life stories, I could write about several theological issues that had been crucial to me and to many other people I knew over the years as well. I wanted to do it for three reasons. First, I wanted to be able to contribute to the ongoing communal theological conversation among God's people about what various Christian doctrines mean and don't mean in our time, especially to many women. Second, I desired to encourage others to join in the conversation, to think about, seek healing, and write about their own lives in the same manner. Finally, I longed especially to write such a book as an act of gratitude to God for the gift of my own life, and for the individual lives of my dear teachers from the early church, for those of my mother and my father, for my aunt, my husband and my children, my students, my friends, and for all those others who share their lives with me.

For a long time my doubts about the project were greater than my confidence that I could or should do it. I told myself that I was a church historian, not, after all, really a theologian. I was afraid I would make a fool of myself. I worried that people would think me egocentric for writing about my own life. I didn't want to seem like a religious fanatic. I wasn't sure that I wanted to say publicly all that I needed to say about the ways in which I had been hurt as a woman within the tradition of the church, and I was concerned that I was getting so far away from my training in objectivity as well as from the early Egyptian monasticism I loved.

In such a frame of mind, I could not bring myself to begin. Then one night, I had a dream. In my dream I was sitting on a shiny black iron bench surrounded by all my luggage in a cool, dimly lit train station in Egypt. Three colleagues who had come to the station with me to see me off were sitting across from me. To my right through an enormous arch I could see and smell the beautiful golden desert I loved, with its dark shadows, its crumbling, columned churches, and the ruined huts of its ancient Christian teachers. To my left were the train tracks running through the station past another huge arch that opened out behind the backs of my waiting companions. Directly in front of me, through this second arch was the place to which I was about to travel. It was a wide field in western Kentucky, my mother's family home. The sky above the field was intensely blue and very high. A dark split-rail fence surrounded the field. In the distance beyond the fence lay soft hills, and just inside the fence a row of tall trees stripped of their leaves for winter. The ground of the field was covered with snow, and there had been an ice storm. Each branch and every twig of trees of that field was clothed in ice, and the ice, which reflected every ray of the sun, shone and twinkled like diamonds.

The next day I began to write these stories.

* *

For being able to follow through with the writing I have many people to thank, the first among them Caroline Walker Bynum, who from the beginning urged me to do this project. She not only helped me frame what I was doing and made useful suggestions about the writing; she reminded me of Madeleine as she encouraged me, metaphorically speaking, not to be afraid of mice, to love winter, snow and ice, and to the tiger in the zoo answer nothing but "pooh, pooh."

I especially want to thank Richard Bondi, my husband, for his support and love, his good cooking, his invaluable help in articulating what I wanted to say, and for his skills and willingness to read and edit the manuscript.

I particularly thank Patrick Henry, the director of the Institute for Ecumenical and Cultural Research in Collegeville, Minnesota, and Margaret O'Gara and Richard Mouw as the joint leaders of our summer groups, but I also thank the other members of the groups for telling their own stories and listening to mine.

Other friends with whom I shared part of what I have written, who have propped me up when I was flagging, and who often made extremely useful suggestions include Terri Bolotin, Bettie Banks, Cynthia Blakeley, Rebecca Chopp, Pam Couture, Gail O'Day, Lauree Hersch-Meyer, Greg Jones, Luke Johnson, Bill Mallard, Melanie May, Sally Purvis, Bruce Robbins, Don Saliers, Melissa Walker, and the sisters of St. Benedict's Convent, St. Joseph, Minnesota.

Finally, it is a pleasure to thank Ulrike Guthrie at Abingdon Press, an excellent, supportive, and patient editor, and a special person to me for a very long time.

◊ ONE ◊

Wearing Away the Heart: Praying to God the Father

Long ago, when I was a little girl living in New York City, every summer my mother, my two little brothers, and I would pack up our suitcases and turn our backs on my Yankee father to take an overnight train to my grandparents' farm in Union County, Kentucky. Once there, we would visit and be visited for part of each day by an enormous assortment of aunts and uncles, great-aunts and uncles, all their children, my first and second cousins, and my great-grandparents as well.

It was an overwhelming experience for an over-serious, shy city child who spent most of the rest of the year in books. So much of it, like taking baths in a tin washtub on the kitchen floor, using the outhouse in the chicken yard, and seeing actual milk coming out of live cows, was exotic. Much of it was intensely boring. The farm rhythms of early rising and early bedtimes, the country distances, and long, silent hours between the relatives' visits made the time in Union County pass with vivid slowness. Aching homesickness for my father made the time go even more slowly.

I always perked up at the beginning of the second week of our visit when it was time for vacation Bible school and revival at Pond Fork Baptist Church, my family's little white frame church out in the fields by the Great Ditch. Every morning for Bible school all the children would gather for country hymns in the old-fashioned sanctuary. Then my class would go for an hour to a little room in the gallery on the second floor at the back of the church for the Bible lessons. Mostly, these consisted of memorizing Bible verses and hearing Old Testament stories of God rescuing children from bad situations—stories of Isaac on the mountain with Abraham, for example, or of Joseph thrown into the pit by his brothers. I also remember one spectacular occasion when my great-aunt Jenny, who was teaching the class, recited the names of all the books of the Old Testament in one breath. I still can see her round face getting redder and redder, her eyes glazing over, and the little spray of spit that appeared toward the latter prophets! At the end of the morning, we would have

Kool-aid and cookies, then finish up with work on some plaster-of-Paris crafts project. It was very satisfying.

Every night, I would come back for the revival with my great-aunts, and this would be a more ambiguous experience. I loved the music; we always sang hymns like "Throw Out the Life Line" and "Revive Us Again" at the tops of our voices, accompanied by a honky-tonk piano. The prayers, on the other hand, were interminable, and there was too much scripture. But the main event was the message—they never called it a sermon. To this I would listen with excitement and dread, leaning, for what safety I could snatch, first against Great-aunt Jenny on one side of me, and then against Great-aunt Nacky on the other.

Brother Smith's message was always the same, and it was not designed for the easy listening of children. "Sinners!" he would shout. "You are all sinners! Are you ready for hell? Do you think you can keep your sins hidden from your heavenly Father? Don't you think your own Father knows what you do in secret? Do you think he can't see into your hearts? That there will be no day of reckoning? Well, I'm here to tell you judgment is coming and it's coming soon! Aren't you afraid?" Soon, I would be huddled down and shivering, not just afraid but terrorized, in my starched sundress between my two big aunts. Brother Smith would go on in this vein for a good long while, then he would shift gears and start preaching John 3:16. "Yes," he would say, "you are a sinner," his voice dropped to a whisper. "But your heavenly Father loves you. He *loves* you enough to send his Son to *die* for you and your sins. Only believe, only believe God loves you, or he'll send you to hell for ever!"

During the altar call, while I sang all the verses of "Just As I Am Without One Plea," I would try my best to flee from the wrath to come by believing that my heavenly Father loved me, sins and all—only I could not believe it. How could God love me in spite of my sins if they were bad enough to make God's own Son die?

After a few days, the revival would be over. We would spend one final week in Union County, and I would take back my yearly allotment of full-color nightmares about God the Father to New York, where they confirmed my ever-growing sense of guilt over the secret rage and grief I felt toward the human father I loved.

The source of my nightmares was the assumption that my heavenly Father was like my earthly father, only more so. My earthly father, whom I worshiped and resented in equal measure, was a remarkable man. He was brilliant, funny, and full of life. He was a loving man, but in those years of his youth, he also tolerated no imperfections or weakness in other people, no laziness, no disobedience from his children or his wife, no sullenness, no arguing with him or asking "why." As for his attitudes toward women and men, he held to an exaggerated version of the cultural stereotypes of the forties and fifties. He only respected men who were highly intelligent and would stand up to him and argue with him. These same qualities in a woman, however, he found contemptible. The woman who won my father's approval could not win his respect. A good woman was sweet and pliant, quiet and obedient. I not only knew I could not be sweet, pliant, quiet, and obedient; I also knew I did not want to be that way. But I had to be! How else could I be, if I were female? I loved my father so much, yet I knew I could never please him. I was angry with him and guilty over my poisonous secret, anger. I could not possibly believe my human father loved me as I was. And if this was true of my earthly father, how much more must this be the case with my heavenly Father. Surely, my heavenly Father's standards for females had to be stricter than my earthly father's.

When I was eleven and a half, shortly after we returned from our summer trip, my parents were suddenly and unexpectedly divorced. Within two months, Mother and I and my two brothers had moved to Kentucky. After that, I saw my father only once a year during a very painful visit.

In the following years of my adolescence, through college, seminary, and into graduate school in England, my feelings and my expectations about my human and my heavenly Father continued to be mixed together. I longed for God, as I longed for my father, but I knew I was not perfect, and I could never figure out how to reconcile all the conflicting expectations they seemed to put on me as a woman. My inadequacies filled me with guilt, and my femaleness overwhelmed me with shame.

Of course, all this affected the rest of my relationships, to myself and my work, to my family, to authority figures, especially if they were male. And almost all of it was tangled up in those bad old days of the fifties and sixties with the cultural expectations, in which the church so richly shared, about women, and their inferiority to men.

As I entered adulthood, I lived out my ambiguities, longings, and helplessness in many ways. I played out my simultaneous attraction and repulsion toward God the Father by going to seminary and the first part of graduate school to study not Christian theology but Hebrew and Old Testament. I had had glimpses in those Old Testament stories in vacation Bible school of a God who did not throw people into outer darkness, where there is wailing and gnashing of teeth. I avoided courses in the New Testament, church history, or theology. I sat in classrooms and tutorials in terror of male teachers and students and the judgments they might pass on me. I worried that there was something wrong with me for wanting to be in those male preserves at all. I tried not to see or think about my human father any more often than I could help; I tried to lay aside the parts of myself that had most suffered in my relationship with my father. As for God, I found that in public prayer, the very use of the name Father would regularly fill me with a sense of inadequacy, helplessness, and depression.

All of this is very interesting, no doubt, but I tell it not because I am so infinitely fascinating. I tell it because in many different versions it is the personal history of so many people—women, and a surprising number of men, too, if you take out the parts about being female. For so many of us the language of God the Father, and our own painful experiences of ourselves and our human fathers are tangled together. So many of us think we have no choice but to cut off great chunks of ourselves as we handle the pain, by either *refusing* to call God father at all, or by using father language without allowing ourselves (or others) to *question* what this language means to us.

How has this situation for so many people come to be? For the early church, being made in the image of God implies a correspondence between ourselves as human beings and God, in which God is the original and human beings are the images. Practically speaking, this means for our Christian ancestors, that, in an unfallen state, if anyone wanted to know what it means to be a human being, we could find out by looking at God. At the same time, they believed, we ought to be able to learn about God by looking at human beings. Because human fatherhood *ought* to be the image of

God's fatherhood, therefore, if we wanted to know what God's fatherhood is truly like, we would find out by looking at our relationships with our own fathers and the people and perhaps the institutions in our lives who stood in the place of fathers for us.

Unfortunately, we do not live in an unfallen world. The primary and earliest place we do learn about fatherhood, human and divine, is from our own fathers, but the fatherhood we learn about is not unfallen fatherhood. In the world of experience, because our own fathers were wounded, even when they long to, they never do perfectly image God's fatherhood. Without even meaning to, and sometimes even trying very hard not to, they have wounded us, their children, by the way they were fathers, just as we wound our own children, and so, without intending to, our fathers pass on a wounded image of God's fatherhood as well.

But even if we have been able to enjoy the blessing of growing up with a human father who does come close to embodying the life-giving qualities of God's fatherhood, none of us is free of the terrible pull of these fallen and destructive images of human fatherhood. Our larger culture still suggests to us fathers are somehow by nature authoritarian and perfectionistic, that they are powerful, dominant over or exploitive of the women in their lives, emotionally distant, stoic in the expression of feelings, more concerned with the abstract than the practical.

Throughout Christian history, like Brother Smith at Pond Fork Baptist Church's revivals, our churches have made it far worse by suggesting that what we experience as the destructive characteristics of a fallen fatherhood are not only *not* destructive, but are truly modeled on God's own self. Through most of Christian history, for example, right into our present time, churches have barred women from ordination, or devalued women if they were ordained, because women were "less" than the full image of God's maleness. But women are not the only ones who have suffered. The churches have used this distorted image of God the Father to shore up the often destructive authority of our institutions, secular as well as sacred, over against the poor and dispossessed, the very people to whom our churches were meant to bring the gospel. We need to recognize our churches' complicity in distorting the image of God the Father, and we need a way out of the impasse in which such a damaged image leaves us.

As for myself, the beginning of my way out came early in the second half of my graduate work at Oxford, as a result of a liberating and life-changing encounter with the tradition of the church itself. I had begun my graduate work in Hebrew and Old Testament. Now, through a number of unlikely circumstances, I found myself in the Bodleian Library unhappily searching for a dissertation topic amongst piles of early Christian texts. Day after day I read page after page of Christian literature, and each page lay as heavy on my heart as Brother Smith's revival messages.

Then, one day, late in a dusty autumn morning well into my despair, I opened in the middle of a book with the unpromising title *The Thirteen Ascetical Homilies of Philoxenus of Mabbug.* It was a collection of homilies written in the tradition of the first great Christian monks of the Egyptian desert. Though I knew nothing of them at the time, I can tell you now that these monks were a puzzling group of people because they were the great heroes of the ancient Christian world at the very same time they challenged everything their world seemed to stand for. By their own lives and teaching, they offered radical Christian alternatives to the ordinary life patterns of the culture—alternatives to the social order, to gender expectations and family, to the uses of money and power, dominance and submission— which the rest of the Christian world took for granted. God's love for humankind was the foundation of their radical Christian vision; our love for God and neighbor was its goal. But I knew nothing of all this, confronted in the library by the *Thirteen Ascetical Homilies.*

Unknown to me as the monks were, however, the contents of that book began to open my eyes at once to another reality, in which I would learn that God was very different from the one I had thought God to be, and that this was going to have immense repercussions for me.

What I read that day was an exhortation to those early monks not to criticize or judge one another, but rather, to treat one another with the gentleness of our heavenly Father, who especially loves the ones the world despises, and who is always so much more willing than human beings to make allowances for sin, because God alone understands our circumstances, the depths of our temptations, and the extent of our sufferings.

I read, and I was astounded. God the Father is gentle and makes allowances? God the Father especially loves the castoffs? What would this mean, if this really were true? Was God really uninterested in sin? Could God the Father expect *less* of me than my human father? Could God the Father *want* and even *like* women the church I knew rejected? I did not then know the answers to these questions, but I knew that somehow these people who lived nearly a millennium and a half ago had spoken to me directly out of their own love, and of God's love for me. I resolved on the spot to spend my scholarly life in the company of those early monastic teachers, and to let them teach me what they could of the God they clearly loved and whom they clearly experienced as loving them as well. And this is what I have done.

Of course, my whole life did not change at once; the monastic teachers themselves insist that God rarely heals in any "all of a sudden" way without a very long back-and-forth movement of God's grace, insight, and our own very hard work. But over the next many years I began to get some glimpses into their understanding of what it means to be Christian that started to turn my view of God's fatherhood upside down.

I discovered first of all that for the monastic teachers humility is the key virtue that is both the starting point and the enabler of the whole Christian experience. What they meant by humility, however, had little to do with the modern, everyday use of the term. For them, humility was not about groveling before God or other human beings. It had nothing to do with being passive, being a doormat, or glorifying having a poor self-image. It was certainly not a virtue recommended to women or poor people so that they would accept their place in society.

No, humility for the ancient teachers meant accepting ourselves and others just as we are, limitations, vulnerabilities, and major imperfections included, as already equally valuable and beloved of God without our having to prove our worth by what we accomplish, what we own, what we do right, or by our status in society and in the church. This meant that humility was about slipping underneath the whole hierarchical social web of judgments by which we limit ourselves and one another in order to love and act fearlessly with power and authority.

The guarantee of this humility for the monastic teachers is that it is grounded in the humility of God, as we meet it in the person of Jesus. Think of it!—the humility of God, who has no need to prove God's power and might over human beings, who absolutely does not desire to dominate us, or bend us to God's will. God the Father? Dimly, I was beginning to see that this person might not be the one I had thought.

I wanted humility. I knew by now, however, that humility was not a virtue the ancient teachers thought human beings acquire all at once by gritting their teeth and becoming humble. Like all the qualities of God's love in which human beings are made to share by virtue of the image of God, humility, they believed, is formed in us as a disposition only over a very long time. A vital part of the process of formation was a daily practice of prayer, including most especially reading and mulling over scripture. Because by now I wanted so badly what they had, the monastic teachers had convinced me that it was worth the risk to try, with their help, to enter into a relationship of daily prayer with this God who was turning out to be so different from the one I had so long thought God was. This is what I did.

Once begun, I was on a journey into a nearly un-known territory. Painfully, over a matter of years, with the monastic teachers' help, I was able to lay aside my modern assumptions about prayer. I gave up the idea that prayer is about finding peace, or about accepting whatever happens in life, no matter how tragic, as the will of God. I abandoned the notion that prayer is

basically verbal, petition and praise, and came to see
that prayer is a sharing of the whole self and an entire
life with God. With a great wrench, I set aside the
conviction that the process of moving closer to God in
prayer should also be a process by which we discard the
damaged parts of ourselves of which we are most
ashamed. I learned instead that just the opposite is true,
that prayer is a process of gathering in and reclaiming
the lost and despised and wounded parts of ourselves,
even those parts that could not speak the word *father*
without suffering and shame.

In short, I discovered for myself that one of the major
works of prayer is ongoing, over-a-lifetime healing, and
some of this healing involves very painful work. One of
the monastic teachers was once asked, "Of all the
virtues, which is the most difficult to practice?" "It is
prayer," he replied, for "prayer is warfare to the last
breath."[1] Prayer, I learned, is warfare to the last breath
because so much of the healing work of prayer involves
gaining knowledge of our own hearts as we strive to
understand our actual feelings, attitudes, convictions,
and motivations. "Not understanding what has happened prevents us from going on to something better,"
the teacher Poemen used to say.[2] Keeping ourselves at
the introspective work of facing "what has happened"

---

1. Agathon 9, in *Sayings of the Desert Fathers*, trans. Benedicta
Ward (Oxford: Mowbray, 1981), pp. 21-22.
2. Poemen 200, *Sayings of the Desert Fathers*, p. 194.

head on in the presence of God can be so hard and so painful that sometimes we would almost rather die than do it. I began this very painful, introspective work of prayer.

It was a long time, however, before I was able to face directly the whole issue of fatherhood in my prayer. At last, however, I had learned two of the most important things about prayer the monastic teachers have to teach. The first is that healing depends upon facing the very thing you find you absolutely cannot face, and doing the very thing you are most certain you cannot do. The second is that, because human beings are related to one another and to God through the image of God, being unable to use a particular name for God means casting off both the human relationship the name signifies, and parts of ourselves as well.

I decided, then, that I must go through a *limited* period in which I would deliberately call God Father in my daily prayer, and ask God to tell me what it meant to call God Father. I prepared to allow the most vulnerable parts of myself to enter into conversation with the one I would call by this name. I knew this was going to be painful and very risky. I had continued all these years to feel judged and rejected by the human father I still grieved for, and it seemed to me that my only chance of controlling the pain was to avoid him and try not to think about it.

As for my heavenly Father, what if I allowed the Father to see all my character flaws and weaknesses, and God responded by leaving me? I knew that the central Christian tradition had insisted that God is not male. At the same time, there has always been a strong voice within the tradition that has suggested that only men can truly be the image of God because they alone are male like God the Father and Jesus. What if God the Father were to tell me that this tradition within the tradition was right, and that I, as a woman, should accept myself as a second-rate human being? That I did not, therefore, belong in a leadership position in the church? In short, that the God I had gradually been getting to know and love was really a figment of my imagination? That God the Father was exactly who I had always feared? How was I going to be able to do such dangerous praying?

One reason I was able to take the risk was that I trusted my monastic teachers. My teachers in fact were called Abbas, or "fathers" by those who had learned from them in the ancient world. In their spiritual father-hood they had deliberately modeled themselves on God in Christ, and they had been the source of so much gentleness, grace, and liberation for me. Could God the Father be so different from them?

I was also able to risk it because from the time I began my daily prayer, I had taken seriously Abba Poemen's advice to Abba John:

The nature of water is soft, that of stone is hard; but if a bottle is hung above the stone, allowing the water to fall drop by drop, it wears away the stone. So it is with the word of God; it is soft and our heart is hard, but the [one] who hears the word of God often, opens his [or her] heart to the fear of God.[3]

Scripture, particularly the psalms, was the very backbone of the prayer of the ancient monastics, and I had tried to model my own prayer on theirs. I could not call God Father. Yet, the hard rock of my fear was being worn down daily by hearing in my heart in scripture a whole set of names for God I had not been able to hear before: faithful one; shelter from the scorching heat, wings of a great bird, sider with the outcast against the powerful; mother, creator, quiet voice, light, love. I was beginning to understand how these names of nurture, life, and gentleness not only *modified* the meaning of the magisterial names of God, like almighty, king, warrior, and judge, but actually seemed to have turned their meaning upside down. Perhaps, I thought, scripture turns the meaning of the name "father" upside down as well.

But scripture had also already begun to wear away my heart in another way, too. Now I knew that, though

---

3. Poemen 183, *Sayings,* Ward, p. 192.

Jesus told us to call God "father," and though the language of "father" hurt me, Jesus is about the business of bringing life to people, not death. Jesus preaches the Kingdom, and he teaches us to pray for the coming of the Kingdom, for the time when our life together and with God will be characterized by its love, and by its freedom from all that keeps us from love. I knew that Jesus was my ally in my struggles, for Jesus does not preach knuckling under to the status quo on any issue. It was the Pharisees who did not like Jesus' healing on the Sabbath, or association with the undesirables, like tax collectors and women. It was Jesus who healed, and associated with the outcasts anyway, and who said continually and was saying to me now, "Be not afraid." Perhaps, I thought, the Father of Jesus may not, in fact, be a God who uses God's authority to demand obedience to the status quo.

So I began my experiment in calling God father. As is true in prayer, some of the insights I had came quickly, and some slowly, in fits and starts, and needed much unraveling over a very long time. It would not be useful to chronicle what came out of that prayer. I would, however, like to pass on three insights from that period that have been extremely helpful to me ever since.

The first of these insights came the day I read in the context of my morning prayer the familiar account of Jesus' conversation with the disciples in John 14. The conversation recounted in this chapter of John takes place after Jesus' final meal with the disciples in which he has washed their feet. Now, he is trying to make them ready for what lies ahead by telling them that he is going to his Father to prepare a place for them. As is often true in the Gospels, the disciples do not understand what he is talking about. "What do you mean, 'prepare a place'?" they ask him. "How will we get there?" "Who is this father?" they ask anxiously, "and what is he like, anyway?" Jesus tells them not to worry. "If you know *me,* you will know my father, also. From now on you do know the [Father] and have *seen* him." "What do you mean?" Philip cries out. "Lord, *show* us the Father, and we will be satisfied." And Jesus answers, "Have I been with you all this time, Philip, and you still do not know me? Whoever has seen *me has* seen the Father. How can you say, 'Show us the Father'?"

"Whoever has seen me *has seen* the Father!" I am an early church historian, and my speciality is in christology, and I have done a lot of work on trinitarian theology, as well, so what I am going to say now is really embarrassing to me. For years I had taught, according to the witness of the whole church through the ages, that Jesus is God among us, completely human and completely God. I had also taught that with respect to the Trinity, the Son is not subordinate to the Father, but fully equal to the Father. Together these two statements clearly mean that if we want to know who God is, we can look to Jesus to find out. Now, I was realizing that, though I had believed this in my *head* and taught it, I had neither believed it in my heart nor understood in my heart the significance of the traditions I was teaching.

What I *had* believed in my heart—as opposed to my head, where I knew better—was what I imagine a lot of us believe, that Jesus was fully God among us when he showed forth the will of the Father in the great universal and symbolic acts of salvation history, from incarnation, through the crucifixion and resurrection, to his final coming. At the everyday, *ordinary* level, however, I was convinced, the human Jesus was not only *subordinate* to the Father; I *actually* thought in my heart that Jesus' rejection of the status quo, his friendship and support of women, and his refusal to be intimidated by religious authority told us nothing about God the Father at all. In other words, for those of you who have been to seminary and remember your church history, for all practical purposes, I had been one of the heretical Arians, who believed that the second person of the Trinity is subordinate to the first.

Now, for the first time, I could see the point of the orthodox insistence that the Son is not subordinate to the Father. I could understand in my heart and in my head what it means to say that if anyone sees Jesus that person *is* seeing the Father. It means, if the human Jesus who is also God does not spend *his* time bossing around his friends, intimidating or demanding obedience from them, then the Father must not demand our unquestioning obedience, or wish to intimidate us, either. It means, if Jesus is not interested in drawing his disciples from among the religious hierarchy of his day, neither is the Father. It means, if Jesus' particular concern was for the healing and empowerment of the poor, the widows, those with loathsome social diseases, and the crooks, so was the Father's. It means, if in the Gospels Jesus' closest friends, Mary and Martha, are women, most certainly *God* the Father does not remotely value women the way my human father, the church, and the larger culture value women.

Indeed, if this is who God the Father is, I discovered, to name God Father in prayer is not to submit to a God who tells us as women to be respectful of the status quo. It is, rather, *to invoke God's fatherhood as a mighty corrective* against all the murderous images of *fallen* fatherhood that hold our hearts and persons, our churches and our world captive. This was my first insight.

Several months later, the second of these insights came to me. I was still pondering Jesus' saying "the one who has seen me has seen the Father" when John 11 turned up in the daily lectionary reading. Until this reading, which we know as the raising of Lazarus, I had heard John 11 as a statement of Jesus' mighty Lordship over death. I had understood the chief character in the story to be Jesus, and the central event, Jesus' powerful summoning of the dead Lazarus from the tomb. Mary and Martha I understood to be secondary characters, whose passive weeping was there only for the contrast with the active Jesus.

The day of my insight, however, it struck me like a blinding light that the powerful Jesus who is God is not, in fact, the only major character in John 11. Rather, Mary and Martha have equal place in the story with Jesus. This is because the story is not so much about Lazarus being raised from the dead as it is about the way Jesus and his friends relate to one another.

You recall the story. It begins in Bethany when Mary and Martha call Jesus to come heal their brother Lazarus, who is dying. With uncharacteristic insensitivity, Jesus does not go until Lazarus has actually died and been in the tomb four days. When Jesus comes, Martha and Mary both confront him openly and even bitterly with their bewilderment and anger. "Where were you when we needed you?" they ask him. "Do you not know that Lazarus' death was completely unnecessary? How could you have betrayed us like this?" Jesus, on his part, does not threaten them for refusing to accept his will, nor does he accuse them of lack of faith. He answers them seriously. Only then, weeping in frustration on the hold death still has on life, does Jesus raise Lazarus from the dead.

This time I heard the story in the context of my pondering on "whoever has seen me has seen the Father." Now, I recognized something else enormously significant I had believed about the meaning of God's fatherhood that I never before had known I believed. In my heart, I had been assuming that when Jesus told us to call God "Father" he had meant that as God's children we were to relate to that Father as *very little* children relate to the kind of benevolent, dominant parent who prefers toddlers to adolescents because toddlers are so sweet and adolescents are so complicated. My whole life had been spent trying to become an adult! I had always known in my heart that I needed to be an adult, and my instinct for self-preservation had been telling me that I could not afford to relate to a Father God who demanded that I live as a helpless child.

Now I could see that I had misunderstood all along. If it is true that "whoever has seen [Jesus] has seen the Father," it is important that in John 11 Jesus gives no sign that he expects Mary and Martha to relate to him as passive, obedient, little children. Martha and Mary are Jesus' *adult friends*. Because they love him, they are not submissive or subservient. They are not in the least afraid of him. They are not sullenly, silently angry with him. They do not accept what has happened as the will of God. They tell him they are angry with him, and why. As for Jesus, Jesus does not simply tolerate these uppity women. He values them. He chooses them for his closest friends. He trusts them in their anger with him, and he trusts them with his life.

This moves me to my third and perhaps most life-transforming insight from praying scripture, which is that God does not simply *value* our friendship. God actually chooses to *need* us. At the beginning of John 12 stands the story of the woman who poured perfume over Jesus' feet. In Mark, this woman is nameless, but in John it is the same Mary we have just met in the preceding chapter. The story begins with Jesus at table with the disciples during Easter week. Jesus is warning them of his coming death, and as usual, they are refusing to listen. Then, Mary comes in and pours the perfume over his feet. "How wasteful!" one of them says. "No," says Jesus. "She is preparing me for my burial." How abandoned Jesus must have felt in his disciples' refusal to listen to his warning about his upcoming death! How much Jesus needed Mary's affirmation of his own fear of death, which we see displayed so painfully in Gethsemane!

Why was Mary able to do this for Jesus? I believe it was because she had an adult friendship with Jesus. She had not backed away from him and obediently accepted her brother's death in chapter 11, but rather she had pushed Jesus and argued with him and held him accountable. Now, as an adult, she was able to see the truth of Jesus' impending death and accept both his fear and her own grief and pain over her coming loss.

Eleven years ago my father's sister, whom I had not seen since childhood, moved to Atlanta, and we began to spend wonderful time together. Throughout my relationship with my ancient Christian teachers, they had been warning me that the work of prayer and healing is not only an internal mental process. It involves work and often major risk in the external world of relationships as well. In the midst of my pondering John 11, my aunt suggested that I go and visit my father, whom I had not seen for a number of years. I knew that he was remarried, that he was ill with emphysema, and that he was retired.

I was terrified by the idea of a visit. I also, however, remembered my monastic teachers' insistence that healing comes not by avoiding but by facing what we are most afraid of facing, and by now I truly trusted my teachers. In fear and trembling, therefore, I took a trip to Connecticut. It was not an easy trip, since I was still so afraid of him. I found, nevertheless, that my new insights about God and my relationship to God made it possible for me to begin to relate to my father not as a little child but as an adult.

And now, amazingly, being able to see him for the first time through adult eyes, I began to be able to see, not my childhood image of my powerful, mythical father, but rather my actual, flesh and blood, real human father. In that trip, I began to learn that my father had changed over the years. He still had a formidable mind, but from somewhere and against all expectation, he himself had learned a great deal of gentleness. Just as surprising, considering his previous history, he had become a Christian to the core.

As I began to visit him regularly, hard as it was at first, knots began to untie within me, and parts of myself long gone started to return. I gave him everything I wrote in those last years, and he always was able to see to the heart of what I had written. I argued with him, for the first time in my life. He told me frequently that he was proud of me. I found that as I no longer needed God to take care of me as I had before, as a little child, so I no longer needed my father to take care of me.

I am not sure at what point I realized that the man whom I had seen as my all-powerful and invincible father not only wanted me as I am, but also needed me to stand by him through the long journey into his own death. My father needed my friendship. It still seems to me to be an astonishing gift of God's grace that in the last years of his life I was able to stand with him as his friend who was his adult child.

This story, like my life, is not yet over, but from where I stand in both I would make some final reflections.

First, I would suggest that none of us can really afford to say, "I cannot cope with my relationship either to my own father or to God the Father; therefore, I will simply set it all aside."

This does not mean, however, that I am offering a dogmatic defense of the use of "Father" language for God in public worship, but rather, it means that I am offering some suggestions for healing the wounds connected with fatherhood that so many of us carry around. Pastors especially have a responsibility to make sure that the language of worship does not hurt people or make God distant. I believe this means both that we must be extremely cautious in the use of Father language and that we must deliberately seek out and strengthen the use of other names and images of God for people who are suffering over "father" language. Some people will never be able to use father language without this language harming them.

At the same time, the work of learning to name God "father" is work that each of us must do in our private prayer. Public prayer may make the work easier or harder, but it will not take the place of our own personal wrestling with God, scripture, and our own hearts.

Second, in the context of this work of prayer, the tradition has, indeed, often been the carrier of fallen images of God's fatherhood. At the heart of the tradition, nevertheless, is the gospel, and the gospel presents an image of fatherhood that stands in judgment over any other image that destroys or belittles anybody, even if that image is conveyed by the tradition itself.

Third, I know now that Brother Smith was wrong all those years ago in the revivals at Pond Fork Baptist Church. We are each one of us infinitely precious to God the Father. God does not love me, or Brother Smith, *in spite of* who we are. God loves us *as* the very people we are. God has chosen to need us, and God longs for our adult friendship.

Finally, God's Fatherhood is not an invitation to have our needs met in exchange for becoming obedient or subservient little children. It is an invitation to stand with God as adult friends of God. It is also only as we can set aside our wounded images of God's fatherhood to accept this invitation to become adult friends of God that we are able to let our human fathers be our actual fathers, neither more nor less than who they really are.

My father is dead now, and I miss him very much. He died this past year on March 28, Holy Thursday, and his funeral was on Holy Saturday in a church already filled with white dogwoods for Easter. As I looked at my father's casket in the front of the church that day, my heart was filled with gratitude for the gift of friendship God had given my father and me in my father's last years. On that Holy Saturday, I knew that the same God who had given that gift now had leaped into the fearsome darkness of death there to meet my father as friend, and to bring him safe into the joy of the Resurrection.

Praise be to the God who creates us and re-creates us, who shows us the meaning of fatherhood in Jesus, who calls us into friendship, and whose names are without number!

Praise be to the one God who speaks continually to our hearts, "Be not afraid!"

◊ T W O ◊

Being Reasonable: What Do the Grown-ups Know?

One wintry Friday morning the year I was in the fourth grade in P.S. 41, I went as usual with the other forty members of my class to the weekly movie in the school auditorium. I liked the school movies and the unusual opportunity they offered for daydreaming. Being about the progress of mankind in industry, one way or another, they were all the same. Moving pistons, spinning vats of dough, crashing looms, and clacking printing presses whirred against a background of speeding music and virile voices. In the shuffly, pencil-scented darkness, I would sink down in my seat with my feet up and my arms around my knees to imagine the presence of a huge man, dressed in a blue overall with red stitching on the pockets, an entire factory in his hands, striding across the mechanized farms of the Great Plains of America into distant hills. The movies made me proud to be a human being.

Expecting nothing unusual this Friday as the lights went out, I squirmed my way down in my seat into my regular knees-up position. The movie of the week was on the mining, processing, and use of coal. Because it would almost certainly have to talk about fossils, I decided to hold off a little on my usual daydreaming. Coal, after all, was made from the compressed bodies of fat, little-headed dinosaurs and giant ferns long dead, from slithering and flying creatures gone forever from the earth. I loved the idea of fossils.

The film had begun wonderfully. By the time we were taken a mile below the earth's crust and into the terrible tunnel to witness an enormous underground drill, my ten-year-old stomach had begun to heave. All of a sudden it had become obvious to me: if coal were only made from plants and animals long gone, there was a limit to how much coal was in the ground. If no more coal could ever be made, then the time would come when there would be no more coal. There would be no more pulsing machines, no more electricity, no big vats of dough. Houses would have no heat; people would have no food. Maybe mothers and fathers would leave their children.

Normally, I was too shy and sullen ever to ask a question in class, but today I could hardly wait for the question and answer time. As soon as the lights came on, I straightened out of my slouch and raised my hand. Immediately, Miss Jason, my teacher, pointed to me and jerked her head in my direction.

"You there, in the fifth row, stand up," she said.

I stood up. "What will happen when the coal runs out?" I asked.

Miss Jason was disconcerted. She looked at me fiercely, the inside corners of her eyebrows touching. "What do you mean?" she answered. "The world will never run out of coal."

"But, Miss Jason," I persisted, the five boroughs of New York City, my home, spreading out before me, dark and empty. "That can't be true if all the dinosaurs are already dead. Sooner or later, we'll have to use up the coal!"

"Sit down right now and be quiet," she ordered. "Be reasonable. Believe me. I am telling you, we will never run out of coal."

I slid back down on my backbone, humiliated and angry, confused and guilty. My questions had gotten me in trouble in school again. I couldn't be reasonable. I couldn't figure out how not to believe what seemed so obvious.

This happened to me all the time. Once, at recess, for example, I came out late to find the girls from my class by the high wire fence at the back of the playground, behind the slides. They were in little clumps, whispering and looking over their shoulders.

"What's going on?" I whispered, too.

"Did you notice Carolyn isn't in school today?" Rosanna, who was precocious, answered. "When Carolyn came home yesterday her mother was lying in the hall and there was blood everywhere and she wouldn't wake up. I know this is true because Carolyn told me she had to clean up all the blood!"

The girls stepped closer together.

"Yes, an ambulance came and they took her to the hospital!" another child, whose name I forget, added. Everyone looked solemn, with the self-importance of knowing something only the adults were supposed to know, and a little frightened, too.

"Where did the blood come from?" I had to ask.

They looked at each other. "We can't figure it out," said Miriam, "but when Carolyn asked her father he got mad and told her to mind her own business. I asked my mother, and all she would tell me is that I'll know when I'm older."

Before we had a chance at further speculation, Miss Jason stomped up to us in her lace-up schoolteacher shoes. She clapped her hands. "All right, girls," she said, "I'm not going to tell you anymore to stop talking about Carolyn's mother. Now get out there and play!"

I never did learn what had happened to Carolyn's mother. I suppose now that she had had a miscarriage, and that she must have lived. At the time, however, the whole thing made me begin to have suspicions about the durability of my own mother. After a few sleepless nights and stomachaches, I finally brought the subject up while Mama was ironing and I was sprinkling clothes. I had thought a lot about the right way to ask my question and had decided not to mention Carolyn's mother at all.

"What will happen to Freddie and me if you die?" I asked.

"Oh," she replied, working on the points of my father's handkerchief, "I won't die till you are an old woman."

"But what if you get sick?" I wanted to know. "What if you have a car crash?"

She set down her iron and looked at me. "I already told you. I'm not going to get sick, and I'm not going to die," she said, firmly.

"But how can you know?" I cried, by this time really anguished.

To which she replied, irritably, with the same answer every mother through the ages has given to the questions she cannot face from her own children. "I just know. That's how! Now, go out and play and get some fresh air." I slunk out in a rage of frustration and anxiety.

As I grew, an increasing number of my questions of this sort were connected with being a female child. Every night after supper, for example, I would help with the dishes while my brother Fred would build things with his erector set. I thought this was terribly unfair. "Why do I have to do the dishes, while Freddie gets to play?" I would ask. I would never have dared ask my father this question. "Because you are a girl and he is a boy," my mother would answer. Everyone seemed to take it for granted that male privilege corresponded to a reasonable law of nature based in female inferiority: my father, probably like every other father in the apartment complex, nightly brought home jokes about pushy and emotional broads at work who couldn't think. The boys in our neighborhood spoke of girls in just the same way: "girls are disgusting; girls are crybabies; girls are dumb."

This was the story of the intellectual life of my childhood. Before I could catch myself I was always making observations or asking questions that didn't fit with what the adults were telling me about the way things were, and I didn't know how to make sense of the differences between the simple answers they gave me and the messy or ambiguous possibilities I saw under my nose. I was certainly smart enough to know that it was unlikely that I would be right about something and the entire adult world wrong, but what was I supposed to do with my own knowledge and experience? I thought I must be crazy. I was afraid of my thought processes, because they got me in trouble and drove people away.

This was also the story of the spiritual life of my childhood. From the summer revival sermons at my grandmother's Pond Fork Baptist Church and my weekly attendance at Calvinistic Sunday schools, I worked out early that there was something about God that made any sort of speculation about God risky. There, I had learned that God said he loved me. But how could I believe God loved me? I was always in trouble with adults for my questions, and God the creator was the power and might behind adult authority. God wanted me to believe what I was told. Indeed, God was so serious about this that God sent Jesus, God's own child, to die on a cross to make me believe. If I believed as God commanded, I would go to heaven. If I sinned by not believing, I would go to hell. I was terrified of Jesus, frightened witless by a God I couldn't believe in, and who asked me not to be who I was, not to know what I knew and who gave me no way to obey.

As I grew into adolescence, these problems did not go away. Indeed, anxiety and guilt about my inability to put aside my own perceptions in order to "believe" on faith and to see things "rationally" only grew worse.

Help seemed to me to be at hand when I fell in love at fourteen with a beautiful blond boy named Herbert. (In those days, love was the answer to a girl's every problem.) Like me, Herbert was in the band and the orchestra—he played French horn, I played flute—and like me, he read books nobody else read and asked questions nobody else asked. He was funny and smart and full of energy. I could hardly take my eyes off him.

The most wonderful thing about him, however, was his family and the way they liked me and welcomed me into it. Both of Herbert's parents had grown up in old New England Unitarian families. His father was an academic scientist, a biochemist who moved purposefully, correcting his sons in the same calm, unanguished voice in which he discussed biochemistry. His mother was an intelligent, decisive, and absolutely no-nonsense woman. She knew everything there was to know about art, music, literature, old movies, psychology, math, and history. She was also able to make anything, including her husband's perfectly tailored sports coats, the sleek, salmon-colored sofas on which they sat in their elegant gray living room, and the delicately beaded silver spoons with which they stirred their coffee.

Unable as I was to escape from the pain, isolation, and guilt of my own intellectual and religious struggles, what Herbert's family had to offer seemed wonderful. What they offered was Reason. This was not reason as it had been defined in my childhood, however—that is, "reason" as what the grown-ups told you anybody with any sense who wanted to be good believed because they were told to believe it. Rather, reason meant logic. It was, literally, no-nonsense. Reason was for the purpose of solving problems and knowing things. Only what could be worked out by the universal laws of logic could be true, and thus real. The laws of modern physics and chemistry were true. Mathematics was true. Human progress was true. Reason was, above all, clean.

The enemy of reason in that household was "traditional religion." Traditional religion was illogical, authoritarian, and impeding of progress, and thus, by definition, not true. This sounded good to me. If I could believe it, in the name of truth and science I could escape the murky and guilt-inducing claims of my childhood God which were so mixed in for me with all the other things I had strained against my own judgment to believe when I was small. In exchange for isolation in the chaos of my tortured, guilty inability to identify the real I would receive a well-structured and shining world of rationality. I would no longer have to live in guilt and ambiguity. I could become an independent thinker.

During the next three years of high school I loved the Taylors more passionately than reason would allow, and I tried my best to embrace the rational as they did. I was

not more than half successful, of course. Faith, even
Enlightenment faith, is never simply the result of the
exercise of logic. The deep beliefs we are called to in
childhood are not abandoned all at once, even if we
never completely accepted them in the first place. At the
same time, observation and reflection on what I could
see for myself continued to make me unable to believe
that life was so transparently, cleanly simple as objective
reason made it out to be. Nevertheless, by the time
Herbert and I broke up when I was seventeen, even with
my doubts, "reason" was what I wanted. I graduated
from high school with an extravagant longing to be
trained in its ways.

College and later seminary were happy to do the job.
The world of the university was populated by a whole
society of people prepared to induct me more fully into
the ethos of "the life of the mind." As it had been for
Herbert's family, the foundation of that ethos was a
commitment to reason, that is, to a model of learning
and knowing based in the logical methodology of the
hard sciences. This was not new.

What I was taught in my classes for the first time was
that reason and emotion were enemies. Where reason
was objective, and universally verifiable, emotion was
dangerously subjective, leading its sufferers to see the
world through their own personal, particular experience. It was only as I could strip away my own emotional responses to particular people or problems that I

could arrive at what was rational. That my own emotions and experience so often stood in opposition to the conclusions of reason did not mean that those conclusions should be re-examined. It meant that my emotions and experience were to be discounted.

At the same time, I was taught to think about the moral life in these same terms. According to Philosophy 101, to be a moral person meant to lay aside the distorting private pulls of pity, preference, and the particular for the sake of the rational and austere sternness of universal law. Ethics was about justice, and justice, like the rationality of which it was an expression, was blind to individual need. Kant, I learned, had said that a person of principle never lied, even in order to save the life of an innocent person, for to fail to tell the truth in every situation meant to open the floodgates of social distrust and chaos.

Soon, in the ethos of the seminary, I would learn how God fit into all this, that is, cleanly, unambiguously, and at a civilized distance. There, it would be suggested to me that God, as the source of the structures of reality, was Universal Reason. God was "the ground of our being" who "accepted us in spite of our unacceptability." But God was not interested in the sins or sufferings of individuals. God's concern was with the human race, and that concern was for social justice. God would no more break the laws of nature for the sake of the inner or outer pain of individuals than would

Kant. Intercessory prayer might do good for the person praying, but it did not move God at all. In fact, intercessory prayer was superstitious, anthropomorphic, and even selfish. God would not miraculously heal people of cancer, or help children find lost dogs.

As for Jesus, he was a far cry from Pond Fork Baptist Church's "personal Lord and Savior" who died to make me believe as I was told. He was Lord, yes, insofar as he showed forth the Kingdom and gave us a perfect example of how to live into it by sharing with us in all significant human experience. But Jesus was only a man. The virgin birth, the miracle stories, the resurrection— all this was merely the mythological language of the early church, from which we needed to extract the universal truth.

I embraced this universal ethos with eagerness. It was so optimistic, and it offered such freedom. It seemed to value asking questions and challenging received truths about the world. Its refusal to take the emotional and the personal seriously promised protection against my fears and anxieties. It was so clean, its answers so unambiguous, so natural. Fear of death? Death is the natural end of life. Guilt over sex? Sex is as natural as eating or mowing the lawn. My murky childhood God who demanded belief was to be replaced with an impartial, rational God who asked only for justice. And what good came out of all this! Not the least of it was the mobilization of my whole class of seminarians in support of the Civil Rights Movement, in many cases against the opposition of their own churches.

On the other hand, even during high school I think I realized that this "objective" way of going about things was actually no more objective than the one I had grown up with. There was so much still that I could not make myself believe. I was still full of questions I couldn't ask, unless I was prepared to be labeled irrational, immature, or even immoral. It took the most fundamental, complex, and subtle human realities and declared them insignificant. But how could I accept death as the natural end of life in the case of a starving child, or a mother dying of breast cancer, frantic for her small children? Even under the best of circumstances, I was unable *not* to know that the reality of death was not clean, universal, simple.

One of the most paralyzingly painful things about this ethos was the way all the claims of objective rationality intertwined with explicit and implicit judgments about what it meant to be female. I began to learn this at the end of the first day of my freshman History of Civilization course. The affable and witty instructor had finished explaining that the course was to be structured around a study of the economic forces that had created the rise and fall of the world's great empires. The insect sounds of early fall came peacefully through the open windows of the sunny room. Now, he stood relaxed, waiting for questions, his pipe in his mouth. A show-off student asked a question about Marx; another asked about factors contributing to Napoleon's downfall. In spite of suffering from elementary school fears of speaking in class, I raised my hand. My stomach hurt. The instructor nodded in my direction.

I tried to articulate my question. "Are we going to study what everyday life was like for ordinary people in each period? I would like to know what they thought about and how they felt about things. Will we be studying that, too?"

The instructor, who was by this time sitting on top of his desk, took his pipe out of his mouth, removed his left ankle from his right knee, looked at me and laughed.

"Just like a woman!" he said. "No wonder women can't think! Women are never interested in the Big Picture; they are so subjective. All they are interested in is feelings! If you want to learn about feelings, go read a women's magazine!" The class laughed.

"Next?" he asked, putting his pipe back in his mouth.

What became increasingly clear in college and seminary was the way the whole scheme of rationality depended upon a hierarchical division of the human race into the "thinkers" and the "feelers." Men were the thinkers, the powerful ones, the objective carriers of the higher powers who thought about the big issues. Women were the feelers, the carriers of emotion, the enemy of rationality, the ones who lived in the realm of everyday, particular experience. What happened in my first history course was repeated in nearly every class in college I ever took. To the questions I increasingly tried not to ask, I received a variant on the same answer: "What kind of a question is that? Women are so subjective!"

Women were not taken seriously because they *couldn't* think. As for women who *wanted* to think, who could not help thinking, these women were contemptible. Women were not *supposed* to want to think. It was the age of the popularization of Freud. Women who thought were told both in university classes and in popular women's magazines that it was the indisputable scientific conclusion of modern psychology that women who thought were unnatural. Smart women made bad mothers. Smart women, like women who were good at sports, threatened, even hurt men.

All this raised two questions. What could I do once I began to suspect that as a woman I would never be more than tolerated in the university and seminary world of rational thought? And even more fundamentally, why in the world had I gone to seminary at all?

From childhood, I had read stories to comfort myself over the messiness of the world. Stories from the Old Testament had given me models of resourceful, independent children God approved of, like Joseph in Egypt, or Ruth. In college I was an English major. Now, recall-

ing my childhood pleasure in Old Testament stories, I
hit upon the idea of writing a graduate dissertation on
the use of Old Testament imagery in the English metaphysical poets. In preparation for this work, one morning I decided to use the summer of 1963 before I began
graduate work to learn some Hebrew at the seminary
on campus. With a little effort that same morning I
talked one of the professors into monitoring me, and
that afternoon I bought a copy of *Learning Hebrew by
the Inductive Method* and a Hebrew Bible.

The next morning I had my coffee, took my books
out of their bag, and laid them on my desk under the
window. I studied chapter 1 of the grammar carefully.
After that, I had another cup of coffee, and I laid the
Hebrew Bible in front of me, opening it, as you do all
Hebrew Bibles, back to front. Then, as I stumbled
through the first words of Genesis 1:1, "In the beginning, God created the heavens and the earth," I had an
epiphany. Why this was so, I do not know, but I still
recall the way the shape of the Hebrew letters and the
look of the light falling on the creamy paper were mixed
up with what I can only call a sense of cosmic goodness
and joy in all created things I had never encountered
before. It was as though the page itself were alive and
the jots and tittles on the letters little flames. For the
first time I could recall, life itself seemed all of a piece
and trustworthy, and there was a place for me in it. In
that instant I knew that God delighted in creation, in

light, in water and mountains, in fruit-bearing trees and grasses, in water creatures and bugs, in wild animals and tame, in men and, most important for me, in women like me.

I decided at that very moment to leave off graduate work in English to do a graduate degree in Hebrew. Within the next few weeks, I applied to seminary for this purpose, and I was given a scholarship. I began second-year Hebrew that fall and I loved it. The next two years I took as many Old Testament and Hebrew courses as I could.

At the same time, the relationship between my study of Hebrew and my understanding and experience of God was far from straightforward. Of course, I was not able to stop believing in God as I had known God until then because what we know of God is always wrapped up in who we are, in our ways of feeling, thinking, and perceiving, as we have been shaped by our personal experience, and by our larger culture. In fact, it was as though I now knew and believed simultaneously in three mutually contradictory Gods.

There was the Christian God I knew from the Calvinistic Sunday schools and Baptist revivals of my childhood who continued to grip my guilty imagination with threats of love, images of judgment, and demands of belief.

Then, there was the liberal God of the world of the university and the seminary, the civilized, distant God of Universal Reason, to whom any attempt to pray in personal terms or for personal reasons was an act of intellectual dishonesty. God in this guise was the very embodiment of all the supposedly male virtues academics including myself admired: rationality, unemotionality, justice, and impartiality. Unfortunately, however, he was at the same time the supreme rejection of "female" emotionality, particularity, partiality, spirituality. ("A fine paper," my seminary teachers would say; "you think like a man.") Belief in this God necessarily entailed the repudiation of myself as female.

Finally, there was the almost secret, private God whom I did not yet know but whom I had first encountered on that summer day in the first pages of my Hebrew Bible.

How was I to live with all this theological mutual contradictoriness? I handled the tension in the way I had been trained in the university: I declared to myself that I was not and would never be a Christian. I simply would choose, rationally, to avoid Christianity. I would not take courses in church history, or New Testament, or theology. Women couldn't think, anyway. I would not grieve for any God I could not please and I could not have. I would spend my life studying Semitic languages, and for two years this is what I did.

Then I went off to Oxford in England to do graduate work in Semitic studies. I thought I had entirely made my escape from my old problems. Oxford, with its women's colleges, took it for granted that women could be scholars. The Oxford program suited me almost perfectly. We wrote Hebrew compositions, both prose and poetry. We studied Semitic philology. We read Hebrew texts and we read few secondary sources. On the other hand, we were not to raise questions about what the texts we studied might really be about.

"Could we take just a few minutes to talk about the meaning of the book of Job?" I asked the last week of a three-term course on the Hebrew text of that book. Embarrassed, the students looked at the table top and shuffled their feet. The Scottish professor drew himself up. "My dear madam," he replied, affronted, "that is something to ask your tutor in the privacy of your own tutorial!" It was at that moment, I believe, that I decided to leave the pain of the present by retreating forever into the romantic dust of the ancient world.

The first warning that things were not ultimately going to work out as I imagined came at the end of my first term. I was sitting tensely in my tutor's office waiting for what came next in his evaluation of my first term's work. He was a small, neat, elderly English Baptist, and he was sitting in meditative silence.

"Well, my dear," he said at last, steepling his tidy fingers, and looking at me with bright eyes. "If you are going to take your examinations in two years, you will need to start your second Semitic language now. Syriac will be just the thing."

"Syriac?" I said, stupidly.

"Yes," he replied. "You will enjoy it. A wonderful language, and all the surviving texts are from the early church!"

I gave him twenty reasons, none of them the real ones, why Syriac with its Christian texts was impossible. In the end, I lost.

I lost badly. Two years later, I discovered that I was actually going to have to do a dissertation in the area of the theology of the early church. The beginning of the search for a topic was truly awful. I spent one anxious week after another in the Bodleian Library reading in Greek and Syriac texts, which soon all ran together in my mind into one. Even apart from the gloom with which these Christian works filled me, I could not get the hang of the way their authors thought. They proved the truth of Christianity by pointing to Jesus' miracles; at the same time, they declared that the image of God in human beings resided in human rationality. In their talk about God the Logos, they seemed to combine in a particularly depressing manner the painfully oppressive language, imagery, and demands of both the God of

Pond Fork Baptist Church and the super-rational God of seminary I had tried to escape.

The beginning of my way out of this morass came about six months into my general reading for a dissertation topic. I had learned that the christological controversies of the fifth century were regarded as central to patristic thought, and that many of these texts were in Syriac. I had begun, therefore, to focus my attention on the writings of the monophysites, one of the major parties in the ancient christological debates. One autumn morning as I sat in the Bodleian Library surrounded by tall piles of nineteenth-century volumes of these monophysite authors, I picked up and opened to the middle of one of these books, *The Thirteen Ascetical Homilies of Philoxenus of Mabbug.*

The homily I opened to that morning was not, however, a christological text. Rather, it was a sermon on the Christian life written in the tradition of the great early founders of Egyptian and Syrian monasticism. It was an exhortation to those early monks not to criticize or judge one another, but rather, to treat one another with the gentleness of God, who especially loves the ones the world despises, and who is always so much more willing than human beings to make allowances for sin, because it is God alone who sees the whole of who we are and who we have been, who understands the depths of our temptations and the extent of our sufferings.

In the reading of those words I was given a second epiphany. I felt my eyes fill with tears of astonishment, gratitude, and hope. Knowing as I did nothing of early monasticism, within five minutes Philoxenus of Mabbug had conveyed to me not only the early monastic *vision* of God, he carried to my alienated and fearful heart the very God of whom he spoke. I had come once again face to face with the elusive God I had met five years earlier in the Hebrew text of Genesis, and for the first time this God was wearing an unmistakably Christian face.

I left the library that morning resolved to do my research on Philoxenus' monastic theology. Unfortunately, this was not to be. Philoxenus was, after all, noted in the ancient world not for his ascetical theology, but for his christology. Even more significantly, however, in the Protestant world of theological scholarship, there was a conviction that the real contribution of the patristic church was made in "the hammering out of doctrine" that took place in the early controversies and ecumenical councils. The early monastic movement was understood to be no more than a backwater of the early church, comprised largely of irrational, body-hating, world-denying crazies who were interested only in the "spiritual life." Serious scholars studied the development of doctrine.

The clean intellectual issues of the christological controversies at this point seemed to me not so much clean as they were sterile alongside the monastic material, but christology was what I was supposed to be doing, and so I did it. At first, everything was straightforward. The christological texts were, in fact, incredibly complex, and in spite of my doubts about whether I could "think like a man" enough to understand them, I enjoyed getting inside the thought patterns of its ancient combatants to make sense of the logic of their theological puzzles. I continued to read widely in the Eastern patristic writers.

Slowly, slowly the fourth, fifth, and sixth centuries began to come into focus. Slowly, slowly I began to learn that the God of the monks was the God of the christological texts. Something was happening to me as my heart began to make connections the university was breaking.

I am not sure at what point I realized I was in a crisis. I only know that one day I woke up with a severe anxiety attack that lasted for weeks. Day after day when I sat down to work, I was paralyzed. I could not read, I could not write, and I could not think. I did not know what was the matter with me. Only gradually it dawned on me. Without even being aware of it, I had committed myself to the God I was encountering in the texts. The problem, now, was that I had also been completely drawn into the logic of patristic christology. I was afraid of my mind that had gotten me in so much trouble in the past. I was terrified that I would find at the end of

my research that all the ancient christology I was studying was basically implausible, and so I would have to
abandon the God to whom I had already committed
myself as implausible as well.

In my paralysis, I did not know what to do. Then,
one day, I brought myself to talk with the chaplain at
Pusey House, whom I knew slightly. He gave no advice,
but seeing that I was suffering from exhaustion, he
offered to arrange a three-day rest for me in the guest
house of the Anglican Benedictine convent off the Iffley
Road in south Oxford. In spite of my rationalistic and
low-church Protestant prejudices, I accepted.

I was in bad shape when I got off the bus at the
Fairacres stop two days later. I barely remember being
welcomed at the front gate and led to the guest house
by a smiling, stout, middle-aged oblate, dressed in a
brown habit. Dimly, I recall her explanation of the rules
of the house and the delicious, comforting smell of food
cooking. I vaguely remember slowly climbing the stairs
to my little room on the second floor, where I shut the
door, lay down, and fell into an immediate sleep on top
of the bed, still dressed in my coat and hat and mittens.

What happened some time later, however, is sharp in
my mind. I was awakened by a knock on my door.
Confused and still in my outdoor clothes, I stood up,
and nearly before I could say "come in," Mother Jane
was in the room. Immediately, her presence over-

whelmed me. She was a tall woman, striking in her graceful habit, and she had a welcoming face with rosy cheeks and very clear eyes, but what was overwhelming wasn't any of that. Rather, it was that before she even spoke I noticed there was something odd about the way she walked, and the way she held herself. There was a freedom in her that I had never seen in any woman, or any living human being, for that matter, a freedom that I had not even *imagined* to be possible. This was a woman, a *woman* radiating intelligence, energy, and kindness, absolutely without fear, completely at home in the world and fully, unapologetically herself.

While I stood there, dumbly, she walked toward me. Then, she bent toward me to give me a kiss. The kiss was too much for me. I threw my arms around her neck, sobbing. She patted me soothingly for a few minutes, then asked me gently what was wrong. Somehow, within a few minutes I gulped out honestly not only all my anxiety about my research, but the fear, and humiliation, and hurt I had felt as a woman around the use of my mind my whole life.

I have never been able to recall her exact answer. I know it was something like, "It is God who gave you your mind; never be afraid to use any of God's gifts to its fullest." But the words themselves weren't so important. It was because like the God of the early monastic writers she had seen me clearly in all my particular pain and guilt, and she had looked on me with love, she was able to free me from my fear. At the same time, because she was a woman who herself so clearly embodied what she said, she showed me that a human being, and a woman, could live in this freedom from fear, full of integrity and joy, her thought, her feelings and her prayer not divided.

In the days that followed, I slept and ate, thought and prayed in a state of peace that I had never known before. As an enclosed order of contemplatives, the sisters had no contact with visitors. In the chapel, however, during the offices of prayer which I was allowed to attend, I watched the sisters attentively as they prayed. I saw them look out the window, listen to the birds, fidget, concentrate, or daydream, and I could see for myself that for them prayer was neither the pious, private, emotional activity that was, as I had been taught, the superstitious opposite of thought, nor was it the rationalistic exercise I had known in seminary. The sisters obviously lived in an intellectual world more real, messier, and less truncated than the one I was trying to live in, and they had the same fearless freedom I had met in Mother Jane.

In Mother Jane and the sisters at the convent I met the same integration of the heart and the mind that I had encountered in the great Eastern teachers of the early church. For Athanasius, Gregory of Nyssa, and Philoxenus of Mabbug, as well as for the teachers of Egyptian desert monasticism, there can be no real split between the spiritual and the intellectual. The reason that this is so lies, ironically, in their insistence, first, that human beings are made in the image of God, and second, that the heart of that image is rationality.

As for the exercise of rationality, for those early Christian teachers, to be rational meant to see the world as it really is, that is, to look on the world, and especially the people in it, with the clear eyes of God. But how does God see the world as it really is? Neither with the eyes of a strict judge whose first concern is for observance of the law, nor with the unemotional, impartial, analytical gaze of the hard scientist seeking abstract universal truth. God looks at the world through the eyes of *love*. If we, therefore, as human beings made in the image of God also want to see reality rationally, that is, as it truly is, then we, too, must learn to look at what we see with love. For the teachers of the early church, rational thought—especially about God or about other people—is only rational when it is also loving.

As for the characteristics of this love, God's rational love is not an abstract, impartial love that looks on all things and all people with the same calm and benign gaze. Of course God's love is universal in that it extends without fail to every single thing, be it plant or person or plateau, God made. This had been part of my discovery of God in the Hebrew text of Genesis.

The beginning of my turning point to Christianity, however, came the day I heard from Philoxenus that only God can judge us because it is only God who can look with compassion on the depth and variety of our individual experience and our suffering, and know us as we really are. For the early monastics, the particular, the realm of difference and experience is not the enemy of rationality. The very trustworthiness of God's rationality depends upon God's seeing and loving particular persons or things as they really are. But if this is true, because we are made in God's image, the trustworthiness of our human knowledge depends upon our ability to see and love the messiness of the particular as well.

The heart of the child, worried that the world would run out of coal, was only strengthened and comforted at last by a woman who said, and demonstrated in her own person, "God gave you your mind; do not be afraid to use it." No longer am I willing to try to trust any form of "reasonable" thought that asks me to set aside my own experience, or my own questions. As a Christian, never again will I try to believe that rationality, love, and the particular can ever be separated.

◊ T H R E E ◊

Some Beautiful Thing: Looking for God Our Mother

I knew I was alone immediately as I awoke in my mother's bed in her tiny condominium on Village Drive where she had lived since she left the big house on Willow Avenue. In a panic, I sat up. Disturbing the darkness of the night, the fluorescent green letters of her digital alarm clock announced 1:37. The blankets were tangled in a knot around my neck and I was wet from head to foot. There was no air in the room. My chest hurt and my heart pounded.

The night before, in the calm, cricket-filled September evening, I had been washing the supper dishes. The phone had rung. School had just begun that week, and my fever of starting-school anxiety was making me clumsy. Water splashed into my face and down my apron as I dropped a dinner plate into the sink to answer the phone.

It had been my brother Fred, calling from Louisville. "Hey, Sis," he had said. "I'm calling about Mom." He paused. "She's in the hospital. I think they're going to do bypass surgery on Monday. She needs you to come on up."

I wouldn't believe it. "What do you mean, 'she's in the hospital'?" I had asked, belligerently. "How do you mean, 'they're going to do bypass surgery'?"

Fred was patiently exasperated. He explained what had happened, what the doctors were saying. I couldn't believe any of it. She wasn't in the hospital. She didn't need surgery. I was angry. I had argued. It was the first week of school. I couldn't leave a class of a hundred and thirty-five students at the beginning of the year. I couldn't come.

He had raised his voice a little. "Roberta," he said, "you have to come."

I arrived at the hospital that evening around seven. On her back in the tall bed, and looking exhausted, she was walled around by my aunts, my two brothers, and half her grandchildren. Surgery had been set for the next morning. We talked on and on about nothing.

Finally, Mama had sent us all home. "I have to ask you to leave. I need to go to sleep," she had said; then, "You children visit each other."

"I love you, Mama," I remember saying before I went.

Fred had let me out at her tiny apartment. In a vacuum of internal silence, I went straight for her bedroom. I wanted to know nothing, to feel nothing. Leaving my suitcase untouched, I stripped off my clothes to drop them on her bentwood rocker. Blindly, I felt for her soft nightgown behind the door and pulled it on over my head. Beside the bed, I had turned off the light in the converted pink milk-glass lamp Mama had studied by as a child. Then I climbed into her high bed, adjusted her pillows, and covered myself with my great-aunt Ginny's wedding-ring quilt. I had said no prayers, falling immediately into a coma of sleep.

Now I was fearsomely awake. My silence was gone. I knew with the force of necessity that my mother was preparing to die. Memories rose in me against my will like waves of nausea: the look of her toes poking through the sides of her old penny loafers as she ironed when I was ten years old; her abandoned face at my grandmother's sink after my father left her; her beautiful table in Louisville when I was sixteen, surrounded by my grandmother, my aunts and great-aunts; the dish-washer she gave me when Anna Grace was born; the piano she bought me while I was working on my dissertation before Benjamin was born. I could not imagine how I could live without my mother, how there could be ground under my feet or air to breathe.

I remembered my own divorce when Anna Grace and Benjamin, my two children, were tiny. Alone, in that first week, twice I had walked through the house, crazed with loss and fear, and heard myself say, "How will I ever support my three children?" Each time I had caught myself. I had two children and a good job. It was Mama, twenty-five years ago, who had been left with three of us, no education, and no job. I was not my mother.

To imagine the world without my mother in it is like conceiving of the darkening of the sun. My life is inseparable from the life of my mother. "Bone of my bone and flesh of my flesh": Adam spoke these words when he first saw Eve, newly formed from his rib. Though they were spoken truly for that pair, they are merely metaphorical for every pair of lovers since. But mothers and children! That is another matter. I am so closely joined to my mother that I am not entirely sure where my mother leaves off and I begin. I am truly formed of the flesh of my mother, bone of her bone.

This shared life with my mother is so complex and so powerful that nothing that I do and nothing that I am falls outside its sphere. This is even true of my life with God, for because of the closeness of my life with my mother, for me to speak only of God as Father is to place this whole realm of my being outside of my identity in God. It is not enough for me to know that I am made, a generic human being, in the image of God who is my Father. I am a woman, and I must know that the image of God in which I am made is also the image of God who is my mother.

Yet it is so hard to think as a modern woman about what it might mean for us to call God "mother," to be made a woman in the image of God. For most of us, the pain of our own experience of being mothered and our sense of failure with respect to our own mothering is so intertwined with our expectations of ourselves that we can hardly even begin sorting out the pieces.

And there is the infinitely complicating factor of fathers and the image of God the Father. For myself, I know that though it was my mother who from my babyhood poured out her life, energy, and imagination over me like water, it was not my mother I wanted to be like as a child, or who occupied my own imagination in my growing up years. I did not want to be a woman, or a mother. Even though I always knew that it was impossible, it was in the image of my powerful father that I wished to be made.

As for God the Father, for most of my life I have only been able to conceive of God in terms of what I have known of my human father. My experience of my father, added to my experiences in my formative years of what the larger culture has decreed about the meaning of "male" and "female" has connected well with the dominant, mostly male images of God passed on by the church, images of God as the Lord God of Power and Might, the Judge, the Ruler of Heaven and Earth, the Perfect One, the One Beyond Need. All this acted together to make my experience of my own mother invisible to me.

How am I to think about what it might be to know God as Mother, and myself in the image of this God? In the following pages I will not start by deciding what mothers ought to be or even are. I am a long way from being able to do that. Rather, I will try to tell the story of my own relationship with my mother over the years. Only then, I believe, as I retrieve my experience of my own mother, will I be able to begin to find the God who is my mother, and myself made in the image of that God, as well.

* *

I remember nothing of Birmingham where I was born, nothing of the short time I lived in Cincinnati with my parents. My first strong memories are in the house of my father's mother in Flushing where we stayed for a few months when we moved to New York. I can still smell the summer air of that house and hear the rattly breathing of the oscillating fan in the high-ceilinged second-floor room which contained my crib, and I feel right now the crisp and bumpy texture of my seersucker pajamas.

As for my mother, I have a few distinct and happy memories of her from this time. I see her smiling at me as I walk beside her on the street, reaching up to hold her hand in a white cotton dress with rickrack and purple flowers she had sewn for me, exactly like hers. I remember a darkened room in which she would rock me and sing the lullaby I heard the whole of my childhood, "If I had the wings of an angel, over these prison walls I would fly." I hear her laughing and talking baby talk to me as she comes up the stairs to get me after my nap.

What I recall of my mother most powerfully, however, was something both more shapeless and more elemental than these specific memories. It was my baby sense that I was only real, only held in existence by my mother's presence. In the hard days of World War II, up-to-date theories of child rearing mandated picking babies up only every four hours to feed them and change them. This way, the theory went, they would not only learn not to cry; they would also become tough and independent. This worked neither for my mother nor for me. I remember my mother telling me how she would stand beside my crib, wringing her hands, crying along with me, and longing to pick me up. As for myself, I remember in a diffused way the quality of my fear, a kind of hunger and a helplessness during those long stretches when my mother wasn't holding me, and I recall in the same way, my sense of myself as whole and real and safe only when I sat on my mother's lap with her arms around me and her enormous brown eyes were looking at me.

In contrast there is a sharp and painful clarity to my first specific memory of my father when I was eighteen months old. I sucked my fingers as a baby, and in those days of scientific child rearing, my father regarded finger sucking as a serious weakness. My father decided it was his responsibility to break me of this disgusting habit. One Saturday afternoon after my nap, I stood, hanging over the top bar in my crib, sucking my fingers and whining a little for my mother to come and get me. It was my daddy, however, and not my mother, who came smiling into my room. I held out my hands to him happily and obediently while he dabbed liquid on my fingers from the little bottle of patent medicine he carried. Its fumes must have made my eyes water, and I rubbed my eyes. The next thing I knew was excruciating physical pain, all intertwined with a cowering bewilderment and shame that my father had hurt me.

Of course, my father had never meant to hurt me like this. In his younger years it was my father's conviction that a father's primary duty was to see to the character development of his children. My mother, he believed, was never strict enough, never loathed tears enough or took the goal of toughness and independence seriously enough. He had not meant to sear my eyes. He had meant to teach me a lesson by burning my mouth when I sucked my fingers.

The trouble was that I did begin to learn a lesson, namely, that in the overall scheme of things, though it was mothers who by their presence held babies in safe and whole existence, the power of fathers to hurt was greater than the power of mothers to love and to hold safe. This was my first baby step toward my inability to picture God as Mother.

The first time I recall thinking self-consciously about what it meant to be a mother in general and my mother in particular came much later, after we had moved to Bayside, New York. It was some time in first grade, and my thinking was prompted by my Dick and Jane reader. "Mother" in my textbook lived in a beautiful brick house, surrounded by a picket fence. In her pictures, she was always smiling, dressed up in a skirt and high heels as she washed dishes, vacuumed, and made cookies for her happy children.

It worried me that my own mother seemed so different from the mother of Dick and Jane. I could accept that Mama had not made a home for us in a brick house with a fence, but rather, in a raw new apartment complex, surrounded with tufts of crabgrass and six-foot oak trees, overrun daily by bands of little boys. What I could not accept was that my mother did not have the same transparency as the mother in my reader. Where Dick and Jane's mother was simple, I could not understand my mother. On the one hand, Mama told me often that she loved being a housewife, that doing housework, sewing, baking cookies, and raising children for the man she loved was the best life possible, and I would love it, too, when I was a woman. On the other hand, my mother sighed a lot, and she frequently seemed sad, withdrawn, or even angry with us children as she went about her work. I didn't know why this was so. Perhaps, I thought, it was because her housework was so hard. Maybe it was because of the baggy old jeans, blouses pinned together with safety pins, and worn loafers she had to wear for it. I only could see that she would never come into focus until 5:30, when she would rush us to put our toys away from the living room, hiding all signs of her own work before she showered and dressed up for my father's return.

If I had asked my mother what was wrong with her in those days, I believe she would have turned aside the question as irrelevant. It was my father to whom she taught us to pay attention, not to her. He was the one who got the first pick of the fried chicken, the perfect piece of pie. He was the one with the infinite supply of funny stories. He was the brilliant one, the one whose approval we all sought and of whose disapproval, scorn, and punishment we were afraid. My father was the bright light of our home, and when he was not there, all of us, even my mother, lived in shadows.

I am not sure when I consciously recognized that all the grown-ups I knew seemed to share my parents' judgment that, while the ways and work of men were significant, the ways and work of women were at best insignificant, at worst laughable. I am sure my clarity grew gradually as I began to think about what it meant that my mother always deferred to my father no matter what he said. I only know that it came to hurt terribly as I realized, when my father told his perpetual dinner table jokes and stories illustrating the stupidity and bad driving habits of women, that he was, by definition, talking about my mother and me. I remember it was around this time that I decided I should have been born a boy. I did not like being a girl; I did not want to be a woman. No man in his right mind would want to be a woman.

This being so, how could I have even known how to conceive of God as mother? In all my memories of my Presbyterian Sunday school and of the revivals at my grandparents' Pond Fork Baptist Church it was the perfect God the Father I heard about. To speak of God as mother would, by definition, have imported all this female imperfection into God. I was afraid of God, and with good reason.

In the spring of the year I turned eleven, the natural order of things began to change when my father set my mother, my two little brothers, and me once and for all outside the godly company of "normal families" by divorcing my mother. In the fifties divorce was a shameful thing. I remember clamping my jaws in rage and humiliation, even six years later, as my high school French teacher, pursing her mouth and patting her hair, would regularly taunt me, "You are just the sort of girl I would expect parents like yours would have."

Who had my godlike father found to be imperfect and therefore rejected to put us in this situation of shame? My grieving and devastated mother, of course, was convinced that it was she, but in spite of what my mother said to the contrary, I believed I knew better. I thought it was my own unworthiness that had driven my father away. I could see that my mother had done all the things a good wife does. My brothers were too little to be responsible. I was the girl who wouldn't be a woman. I was the bad one who secretly refused to accept who I had to be.

As for my mother, I suspect that, if she had known what I was thinking, my tortuous reasoning would have been incomprehensible to her. For thirteen years Mama had seen herself as a good wife: she had cleaned and scrubbed, cooked and sewn, doted and obeyed. She was only thirty-four, and she was still beautiful. My mother may have been grieving, and she may have been in disgrace, but she was not about to lie down in it. Disgrace was not something Mama could directly address, but away from my father, my mother was never a passive person. Mama was not about to give over her life or ours, either. She was ambitious for her children; she wanted us "to amount to something." First, however, she had to figure out how she could support us.

To think it over, as well as to have a place to stay, she took us back to my grandparents' farm in Union County, Kentucky. It was not an easy year for any of us. I longed for my father, feared my big, teasing uncles, and cringed away in disgust and incomprehension from the world of women my mother's enormous matriarchal family inhabited. Everybody treated my mother as a woman suffering from a terminal illness. She was handled gently, yet no one would speak to her openly of her divorce and her divorced status. This does not, however, mean that she wasn't discussed behind her back. I was always overhearing shaming snatches of my great-aunts' conversation: "Mary-Ginny looks terrible." "It's a shame; just a shame." "He ought to be taken out behind the barn and shot." "Her life is just over." "Think of those children." "Such a young woman."

At the end of a year, my mother knew what she wanted. My great-aunt Blacky in Union County and a cousin in Louisville we called Aunt Dorothy helped us move to the city, to a tiny apartment in the Highlands. Aunt Nacky provided a little money for Mama to take a brush-up course in secretarial skills. Within a few months our life was entirely different from what it had been before. Mother had started work as a secretary for the Chamber of Commerce, my baby brother Wesley was in nursery school, Fred was in I. M. Bloom Elementary School, and, miraculously, I was playing flute in the Barrett Jr. High Band.

Perhaps it was my playing in the band that most symbolizes for me the beginning of the change in the relationship of my mother and me in our new life. Once long ago in the sixth grade, before my parents were divorced, I had gone for the first time to a children's concert. There, I had been entranced and astounded by the beauty and emotion and the sheer quantity of sound in the music from "Peter and the Wolf" and "Hansel and Gretel." I still remember sitting dazed during intermission, thinking that all I would need in life to be happy was to be able to make music like that. I rushed home afterward, to try to explain why I wanted a piano, an instrument to play in an orchestra, and music lessons. My mother herself is not musical, but she had understood the precise nature of my excitement and she had encouraged me, warning only that she would have to check with my father when he got home. Daddy had said no. He was angry. "She never finishes anything she starts," he had said to Mama with disgust, as though I were not even there. "She won't do her school work. You know she wouldn't practice, and she certainly would never become a professional. It would be a complete waste of time and money." My mama, to my knowledge, had not argued, and that was the end of it.

So it really did seem to me to be a miracle that within the first month after we moved to my grandmother's farm in Kentucky, my mother had bucked my father's judgment entirely. While Mama was flat broke and still in the worst throes of her own pain, I found myself admiring with awe the three pieces of my gleaming silver flute as they lay embedded in beautiful dark blue velvet inside a new case. The week before, Mama had already found me an upright piano, and I had begun piano lessons with her own old teacher, Miss Charlene.

Of course, I never proved my father wrong about myself and my music. I had no desire to be a professional; I couldn't even imagine growing up. But from the time I began taking piano and flute lessons I played a long time every day, and in spite of hardly ever actually practicing, music was to me almost what I had hoped. I say "almost" because, in my failure to practice, I also never forgot what my father had said, and I was ashamed. My mother, however, did not seem to mind my lack of practicing. She understood that I could speak with the piano and with my flute what I could not speak with my voice.

In the year we moved to Louisville, I think I began to associate my mother's providing for my music with what she was teaching me in general about the saving value of beauty. In significant ways, without enough money to know that we could pay our bills each month, our family lived on the very edge of chaos. Even at the time it seemed to me that in some amazing way, by her sheer insistence upon creating for us a beautiful environment, my mother dragged us far enough away from the mouth of the pit that we were able to live. This she did not do, however, in any conventional sense.

By the end of our first year in Louisville, Mama had found an old, high-ceilinged, two-bedroom duplex on Bonnycastle Avenue. There were no cabinets in the kitchen, and the bathroom was a mess, but there was a fireplace in the soft green living room, wide, dark woodwork everywhere, and bright windows.

In the fifties when the "modern" was in style, and "Victorian" was loathed as fussy, it was nineteenth-century antiques my mother wanted. As for our furniture, she got it from the most amazing places. How she talked her way into the country barns of so many strangers, I can't imagine. I only know that on occasional Saturdays, accompanied by one or more of my aunts and great-aunts, Mother would disappear for a few hours, to come home full of herself, with what appeared to be broken-down, straw-covered, blackened hunks of old furniture nobody in their right mind could want. Then she would cart the stuff off to an old man who refinished furniture behind his house, and, a few weeks later, back to our house it would come, a graceful love seat, a comfortable couch with lovely curved arms, or a carved chest.

Just as no one wanted the furniture of the Victorians in those days, nobody wanted the smaller memorials of their lives, either. Soon, by visiting local auctions, antique shops, and yard sales, my mother had spread before us in the presence of our poverty a beautiful table of old silver plate, cut glass, and china.

In the past, I sometimes wondered how my mother knew to do all this. Now I can see that it took far more than knowledge. It took a kind of extravagant valuing of beauty over what most people would regard as necessities. Though other people were far poorer than we, in our household there was no spare money. I was well into my adult life before I found out how she paid for these things she bought. I was considering buying some beautiful thing myself while I was a married student living off a scholarship and the income from a part-time job. "Go ahead and buy it and eat beans," my mother said. "You can always make do with food. That's why I used to skip supper a lot when you children were growing up."

But there was more to it than that. I don't believe there was one thing my mother brought home over the years that did not evoke her imagination and tenderness toward the everyday details of the life of its former owner. Through these objects that became a part of our household, my mother loved all sorts of people, long dead, whom she would never in this world know. It seemed to me that, as with her brown eyes she had once held me in existence, now by the very strength of her love and her attention she held in existence the intimate, often mundane memories of otherwise forgotten old ladies and children, young men and wives. So, my mother created a home of beauty for us.

With all this, how could I not now see God as my mother as well as my father? I still could not. Whatever else I would have wanted to say about God in those days, I had learned well in church that God was not only All Powerful; God in his shining perfection is in need of nothing. My mother was most definitely not beyond all need. My mama's life as a divorced woman appeared to me to be humiliatingly, messily, hard. This fact alone meant that I could never have seen God as mother.

The hardness of my mother's life filled me with anguish. However early I would awake in the bedroom I shared with her, the house would be full of the sound of the washing machine, the creak of the ironing board, or the clatter of dishes. At 7:15, she would leave for work, harried and beautiful in office clothes, to drop off Wesley at nursery school. Arriving home again, bone-tired at 6:00, there would still be a meal to cook and children to attend to. Eleven o'clock, when I went to sleep, she was still awake, sitting in a patched-together bathrobe at the dining room table, paying bills or sewing me dresses.

The paying of those bills was never taken for granted in our household. Nothing was ever bought in our household without my mother's anxious questioning: "Are you sure you have to have it? Are you sure you can't do without it?" As for myself, I was never able to answer these questions simply. I was too consumed with anger at my mother that my father had left us. Fear that my own future would inevitably be the same as my mother's competed with embarrassment that I was different from my friends with ordinary families, and guilt that I was making my mother's impossible life harder by needing, much less wanting things. And over all the rest, lay a gnawing anxiety over what would happen if we could not pay our bills.

In order to help a little bit with money and to remove some of the pressure of guilt, the year I turned fifteen I got an after-school job as a sales clerk at Grant's, a kind of precursor to K-Mart, in downtown Louisville. Apart from the management, from the teen-aged children to the old women ready to retire, Grant's was staffed almost entirely by women like my mother, who, without men, were trying to support families of children or aged parents. I remember Celia, especially, who worked with me on the jewelry counter. Her fireman husband had gotten into some trouble with the boys at the firehouse. While he was in jail, she worked at Grant's for seventy-five cents an hour. Most of the time she was half-frantic with worry for her little children, whom she left with her in-laws while she worked.

This women's work of standing in the same spot all day on a concrete floor and selling things was boring, and it was physically hard. It was not, however, the kind of work that builds muscles, but the other kind that wears the body out and makes it old. I will always dream, I suppose, of the bodies of the women I worked with, drab with lower back pain and bunions, sagging and straightening, sagging and straightening in the cages of their counters, as they perpetually dusted the same merchandise, the spiffy young manager in his tie walking freely through the wide aisles to make sure no weary woman leaned against the counter.

For financial well-being and an accepted place in society, a woman had to have a man. Without one, a woman had to expect to live hand-to-mouth, a perpetual outsider. The justification for this was straightforward enough. In those years of the fifties, when Freud reigned and "normal" was both a moral and a psychological judgment, only husband-centered, middle-class family life was regarded as "normal." Working at Grant's forced me to see beyond my mother's individual situation so that I learned how society was set up to support the normal and to punish the abnormal. Single women, divorced women, and especially women without men who were supporting families of children or aged relatives were abnormal. My mother's secretarial salary was in line with the Grant's salaries: both were punishingly low.

My mother's advice for avoiding her own financial and social lot was ironically twofold: get an education so that I could teach elementary or high school in order that I might never be financially dependent on a man as she had been, and get married. I didn't want to teach and I didn't want to get married. I didn't want to work with children. Teaching was second-rate, women's work. As my father used to say, "Those who can, do; those who can't, teach."

As for marriage, whatever it had to offer in social respectability and security, I could not imagine myself knuckling under to it. I knew that marriage was not a matter of two equals coming together to share a common life; even in the marriage ceremony itself women had to promise to "love, honor and obey," where men only promised to "love, honor and cherish." It is true that my mother usually described her own past marriage to my father in rosy terms. When she talked about *my* imagined future life, however, she did not bother to romanticize marriage. For my mother, marriage was a kind of servitude necessary to women. "Roberta," she used to say, "you must marry a man smarter than you are. Then, at least you can respect him, since you'll have to do what he tells you."

Nevertheless, with all my reservations about teaching and marriage, I had come to want to meet the expectations of the mother whom I had cost so much. I took my mother's advice. With respect to my education, I could see that my hope for the future lay in my ability to support myself. As for marriage, I knew the advice she had given me to marry was not idiosyncratic. In the Freudian fifties, when a woman without a man was regarded as defective, very few women would really have considered it possible to choose not to marry.

I left home at seventeen to begin what turned out to be a very long process of higher education. The real end of life in my mother's house, however, came with the beginning of my marriage at the end of my first year of college. I was married at eighteen to a boy barely twenty-one who reminded me of my father, who would "allow" me to continue my education, and who seemed smarter than I, so that, as Mama had told me, I could at least respect him when I had to do what he said. That he felt injured by and even loathed the many parts of me that he didn't understand seemed only reasonable. It served me right.

The beginning of my marriage was also the end of my music. My music had been my consolation and my voice, but, as my father had predicted with a force that ensured its coming true, I had never practiced, and I had never become good at it. I didn't deserve it. Now, it was time to shut up. I had already left my piano at home.

Shortly after I married, I sold my flute to the younger sister of a high school friend.

The next years were lonely and exhausting. Not surprisingly, my marriage was difficult. I finished college, went to seminary, and then I went with my husband overseas to graduate school at Oxford, to study first, Hebrew, then early church history. At the end of three years I returned to the States to complete my dissertation while my husband began his teaching career, and in the middle of my dissertation my daughter was born. Five years later, the year after the dissertation was finished and the first year I was teaching full time, my son was born.

Professionally, these were hard years. I had, indeed, chosen a career in education as my mother had recommended, but it was in college teaching, not secondary education. In 1970, the year I began, college teaching was a man's world of privilege. Though I had a classical training in some rigorous disciplines, I still heard the general stuff I had heard right through childhood and into college and graduate school about women not being able to think. Now I also heard, "A woman who teaches is taking a job away from a man trying to support his family," and, "Hire a woman and she will always be out of work with female problems or having babies." Even at school, before anything else, a woman was a wife. I remember one of my priest-colleagues being asked once if he thought women should be allowed to teach college. He paused, thoughtfully, before he spoke.

"Yes, I suppose so," he said, "if it is okay with their husbands and they are able to get their work done at home, first."

Though I enjoyed my teaching very much, I found myself helpless and unable internally to speak against all of this. I had felt obligated over the years to try to prove myself a good woman by putting the same kind of energy into the home that I would have if I had not been a student and then a teacher. Now I also tried to prove to my colleagues at school that a woman can think like a man by continuing the very technical research I did in church history. And, so that no one could use me as an excuse not to hire other women, I missed only one day of school when Benjamin was born.

The problem was that I angered many people just by being who I was, and I could not find any way to defend myself. A lot of this was because women like me who stuck up for themselves in those days were regarded, by definition, as man-hating perverts, wrong in the very act of self defense. Even worse, however, was that I could not simply know that the people who scorned me were wrong. I was deeply divided against myself. Part of me was as enraged over my supposed female inferiority as I had ever been as a child, but at least as large a part of me believed, and continued to repeat to my heart, every negative thing I had ever heard about being female.

As for my mother, for me she was always there, the one against whom I continued to measure myself, and the one whose support and appreciation now mattered to me the most. During the early years of my marriage, my education, and my teaching, she responded with the painfully ambiguous messages of my childhood. She wanted my education, but she expected me to be a wife first, and in the years of my young womanhood the state of my refrigerator truly caused suffering to my mother, and so, to me, as well.

By the time Anna Grace was born, however, amazingly, my mother's vision of what was right for her daughter had begun to change. Perhaps her years of living independently from men had taught her that women can take care of themselves; perhaps it was her observation of my marriage. "Women can do anything men can do! Look at your great-aunts and your great-grandmother and your grandmother!" Mama used to say, and increasingly, "Stand up for yourself! That husband of yours ought to help you out at home; after all, you work as hard as he does!" She had always sewn me pretty clothes; now she stepped up her sewing to make me a professional wardrobe. She bought me a dishwasher, and, most important of all, the year I finished my dissertation, she gave me a piano.

Over the years, gradually, I began to see and experience things differently, too. When Benjamin was a baby, I was divorced, and I did not have to re-enact my mother's life following the end of her own marriage. In the next year I came to a new teaching job at Candler in Atlanta where there was a real commitment to women on the faculty. I remarried—a loving man who really did believe in the equality of men and women and who actually liked the very person I was. I reflected deeply on what Paul meant when he spoke of our equality in Christ. I also began in earnest my work on the early monastic teachers, whose writings in graduate school had first introduced me to the God I know today.

At the same time, while I continued to suffer a lot of self-doubts, my lifelong anger over the whole business of being female had begun to subside. Though an offhand negative comment by one of my male colleagues or students would cut me to the heart and leave me feeling helpless and panicky for a few days, I knew better in my head. My theology and my self-image were far better than that.

Then, one day, after a few years of all this, everything was turned upside down, and I discovered that within myself, very little had changed. I had learned to pray from the ancient monastics I study, and they had been warning me all along that prayer is "warfare to the last breath." I found out what they meant.

The form of daily prayer I learned from them is based in the psalms, and for years this prayer had been life-giving to me. Now, without warning, in the middle of a perfectly ordinary summer, those familiar psalms had turned on me. One day when I sat down at my desk to pray I had found myself unexpectedly assaulted in the psalms by a violent male world. Male images of God subduing the nations, male images of the psalmists whose sons God would multiply like arrows in a quiver, male images of the warrior Israel, of the nations, even of the angels, all rose up to mow me down and crush me underfoot.

I remember from that first day my sense of outrage and betrayal, but the first day was not the worst. By the third morning, with the very act of opening the Psalter I would begin to weep. Day after day I would sit down to pray those psalms, and each day was more terrible than the last. The whole of Christianity presented itself, not so much to my mind as to my very body, as a closed male universe peopled by a male God, a male clergy, and a whole church full of male theologians, with no place in it for women at all!

"I am a church historian. I knew all this before," I reproached myself in anguish, tears falling on the pages of the book. "Why didn't I really understand it?"

At that point, though I longed to throw the Bible on the floor and quit, I continued to pray the psalms. The ancient monastic teachers from whom I learned my ways of prayer had taught me the importance of persistence in prayer, especially at its most painful, for they believed the very pain is a mark of the seriousness of the work being done in us. I no longer trusted the God I had come to know through the psalms and through my teachers. I did, however, still trust my teachers, and so I prayed on, not passively, but bringing into the process every bit of knowledge, intelligence, and self-understanding I had to help me make sense of what was happening to me.

Then came the day I could take no more. I was exhausted by my prayer, worn out with what felt like the struggles of my whole life. That morning, as soon as I opened my Bible I slammed it shut again. "All right, God," I said. "All this is hopeless. You made me a woman and put me in your male world. If you will help me, help me. I give up." I shut my eyes in silence and despair.

And then, gradually, behind my closed eyes, I became aware that I was looking at a living landscape. An enormous shaggy oak tree occupied the middle of my vision. Under it were thousands of animals arranged in a line, and I knew that they were all the animals of the earth. The biggest were closest to the trunk, the smallest under the farthest branches. In the center, under the tree and surrounded by the animals, was a tall, dignified woman, dressed all in brown. She was self-possessed and graceful. Her face was something like my mother's, and her serious and intelligent brown eyes were looking directly into mine. Gradually, as I looked I became aware in my inmost ears of a voice that spoke these words: "This, too, is the image of God."

"The image of God!" Immediately I was filled with amazement and delight. It was true. In spite of all my difficulties, I had not even known before that I hadn't believed I was made in the image of God. Now, for the first time, I *knew* it to be true. I, as a woman—neither as a defective male nor as a generic human being, but as a woman—am made in the image of God. I no longer felt divided against myself. I could be a woman. I was overwhelmed with relief and gratitude.

It was a turning point in my life. As a church historian, I well knew that some of the most beautiful literature of the early church used female images to describe God,[1] and I loved Julian of Norwich, who drew on a solid medieval theological tradition to speak of

---

1. See Homily 46,3 of *The Macarian Homilies* in *Intoxicated by God,* trans. George Maloney (Denville, N.J.: Dimension Books, 1978), pp. 212-31, for one of the nicest examples from the early church. Female imagery for God is common in the great fourth-century Syrian poet and theologian Ephrem; see, for example, hymns 5 and 21 of the Hymns of Nativity, Ephrem the Syrian: Hymns, trans. Kathleen McVey, Classics of Western Spirituality (Mahwah, N.J.: Paulist Press, 1989). The Holy Spirit is often feminine in Syrian writings through the fourth century.

Jesus' loving mothering of his people.[2] As a feminist theologian, I had read a great deal of modern writings about God as mother, and I was committed to speaking this way on principle. It had not been clear to me, however, why such language had not helped my prayer, but rather, had filled me with a sense of grief and loss. Now I understood the reason for my grief. To know myself as a woman in the image of God, to know God as Mother, and to know my own mother as a window into God: these three are inseparable. If one is implausible, to the heart, the other two are, as well.

I know now that God is my mother as surely—perhaps more surely—than I know my own body. As Mary Virginia, my mother, bore me, and as a baby held me and still holds me in being with her eyes and her arms, so does God our mother hold both of us in existence with a steadfast attention so loving and so persistent that we can never escape it, even if we wish.

It has always been the deepest of mysteries to me that my mother has an intimate knowledge of me as a baby and as child that I myself can never have access to at all. It is as though a fundamental part of me has existence only in my mother's memory, and when my mother dies this part of me will die, too. In the same

---

2. See the Fourteenth Revelation of the Long Text, particularly chapters 57-63. *Julian of Norwich: Showings,* trans. Edmund Colledge, O.S.A., and James Walsh, S.J., Classics of Western Spirituality (Mahwah, N.J.: Paulist Press, 1978).

way, God my mother holds the whole of me forever in God's ever-present memory, and God will never die.

At the same time, it is not only myself Mama holds in memory. In a different way, by gathering up and incorporating in her own house the left-behind objects of the lives of ordinary people she has never known, it has always seemed to me that my mother acknowledges and honors the significance of those everyday lives long gone. So, by remembering and incorporating into God's household each detail of the lives of us all, does God our mother also honor and rescue from death those whose lives society has regarded as insignificant.

One of my mother's most amazing characteristics is the way she has always valued and created beauty, even at a time in her life when such valuing seemed to threaten survival. In this, too, I know my mother to be the image of God. Not only has God created all things beautiful from nothing; this is no more than we would expect. In those country barns, my mother recognized broken pieces of furniture for what they were and she paid for their re-creation by going hungry. In the same way, God our mother recognizes the beauty within all the broken and discarded parts of ourselves; and, if we can believe scripture, for our repair and re-creation God pays everything God has.

I was wrong all those years to believe that God looked at the world with the eyes of a culture who did not value women like my mother and me. It was I who had been looking at God through the eyes of the culture, and so at myself as a woman in the image of God as well.

> "God created humankind in God's image,
> in the image of God God created them;
> male and female God created them."

Thanks be to God for the gift that illumined this text plainly to me.

* *

My mother survived her surgery, though I was not convinced that she would recover for a very long time. In November, on my birthday, two months after her operation, I went out and bought myself a flute. In January, I once again began lessons. And in the late spring, I received a box in the mail. She had made me a flowered dress for Easter just like hers. I was proud to wear it, and I looked beautiful.

◊ FOUR ◊

Out of the Green-Tiled Bathroom: Crucifixion

When the children were still in elementary school, three years after I married Richard and four years after I began to teach church history in the seminary, as I was walking between the living room and dining room one day I discovered that I had lost the meaning of the crucifixion. I don't mean that I didn't know what Christians said about the cross. As a historian and teacher of Christian thought, I had a lot more information than most people have, and I knew that. I don't mean that I had lost my faith. It was much stranger than that, something more like what I would imagine a stroke victim experiences when she looks at a familiar object like a book or a dinner plate in an ordinary setting, and can't understand what she is seeing. On that day I looked at the cross, and it made no sense. All at once the crucifixion had become as opaque to my heart as the water of a muddy pond in a forgotten field.

This was a frightening experience. "What is happening to me?" I wondered to myself. "How can I not know what the crucifixion is about when I teach it every day? Have I forgotten what it means, or have I somehow lost its meaning by taking it for granted?" I remembered my grandfather Joe who had begun to become senile in his fifties. "Perhaps," I thought, "this is happening to me, too." I did not know what to do.

At that time I had no regular practice of prayer, but I prayed in my fear, anyway, "Please, God, tell me again, what is the reason for the crucifixion?" Over the following week my confusion and bafflement only grew as I continued to pray.

Then, on the eighth night I had a terrifying dream. I dreamed I was with Richard in my great-aunt Blacky's farmhouse on the hill outside Morganfield, Kentucky. It was the middle of a good-smelling early summer day, with the insects humming and the hassock fan whirring on the front porch. Sunlight poured through the kitchen into the back hall where I stood, but I was in darkness. I was sobbing and wringing my hands outside her green-tiled bathroom. In the bathroom Richard was kneeling in the bathtub, his neck held over the drain by a powerful looking, dark-haired man with a huge knife I knew had come to kill me. "Don't hurt her," Richard was saying. "Take me; just don't hurt her; take me."

In my dream I was dying with grief. I wanted to shout, "No, no; I'm here, leave Richard alone," but I couldn't make any sound. As I watched in horror, the killer slit Richard's throat and red blood flowed all over the green tiles.

Then the dream was over, and I began to rise out of sleep, shivering, sobbing, and covered with sweat. I became aware that Richard was shaking me, petting me, and calling me by name. At once I remembered my prayer, shuddering with horror. In the very same instant the words formed in my mind, "this is what you've always thought the crucifixion is about, but this is not it," and I knew that both were true.

I could not imagine what had happened to me. How could I have not known that I had believed such terrible things? I had liked to think of myself as a fairly simple, straightforward person. Even so, I was always aware that I was not so simple. I may have always held my chosen, adult convictions firmly and fiercely. Still, I knew perfectly well that a good bit of my adolescent and adult life had been governed, not by what I *wanted* to think, but rather by a whole world of childhood and even adult experiences that I often could no longer even remember. These experiences had led my heart to believe the exact opposite of my chosen convictions. Being human, therefore, I had spent a lot of my life full of vague guilt and a sense that whatever I did, it was always wrong—my own version of Paul's paralyzing troubles— "The good that I would do I do not; that which I hate I do."

The only way I knew then and still know out of this trap is to try to discover what my heart believes so that I can argue with it and seek its healing. Dreams and prayer are unlike each other in many ways, but one great gift they both bring is an ability to strip away the whole accretion of our conscious, chosen thought. Then, if we are brave and if we wish it, we are able to look into our own hearts and find, not what we think we believe, but what we really and truly do believe about life, about ourselves, and God. My dream had done this for me. Even in those first waking moments I could see that my nightmare had presented me with an exaggerated and extended image of what I actually had believed in my heart about the crucifixion until that night.

But what on earth had I believed? In spite of myself, since childhood I had always known that I had thought of the work of Christ in terms of sacrifice for sin, but had this meant to me that the crucifixion of Jesus was like the terrible murder in my place of Richard in Aunt Blacky's green bathroom? Did I believe my sin was the cause of Jesus' murder, and if so, what did I think my sin was? Did I believe that, all things being equal, God would have preferred that I be murdered instead? Who was Jesus in all this, and how did he participate? Who did I think it was who had chosen that murder as a remedy for sin? Was it Jesus? Was it God or the devil, or were they the same person? What awful thing was my dream telling me I had been thinking about God?

As embarrassing and as painful as it was, I knew I had no option but to untangle it piece by piece, and over the next year I began the work of doing just this. The following day I began on the long process of recovering and understanding my memories.

I began with the first time I ever heard the words *sin, Jesus,* and *sacrifice* spoken together. It was during a revival at Pond Fork Baptist Church, which I attended every summer when we would visit my relatives in Union County, Kentucky. As I have said already, Pond Fork had always been the church of the oldest generation of my mother's family. Set in the middle of the corn fields out by the Big Ditch between my great-grandparents' farm and my Uncle Bob's, it was a little church, an old-fashioned, white frame building with a gallery and a potbellied stove.

In the days of my childhood, the summer revival was the high point of the church year, and it was not only a liturgical event. It was an occasion out of the ordinary, like the Union County fair or the Fourth of July picnics. Like the picnics and the carnivals at the fair, there was something about revivals that was dangerous, something that threatened what my polite family everywhere else regarded as socially acceptable. During revival meetings other families' grown-ups sometimes sobbed and shouted and said things I knew they shouldn't in the presence of children. The pushing-the-limits kind of danger at a revival had the same questionable quality to it as the jokes my uncles sometimes told at our enormous family dinners. Though I never understood them, I could tell that they were important because they made my aunts who were waiting on the table angry and blushing.

The goal of a revival was to create or revive in everybody the threefold conviction that each of us was so rotten to the core that we deserved to die and roast in hell forever; that God was enraged enough at us to kill us; and finally, that, in spite of everything, God loved us enough to rescue us by sending his son as a sacrifice to die in our place. As for how Jesus himself saw all this, it was just fine with him. To die for sin in perfect obedience to the will of the Father was the only reason he had been born in the first place.

Not just the preaching but the whole service was aimed at convicting us of the truth of all this. Before Brother Smith ever began his message of sin, hell, and love, we were already well prepared. To the accompaniment of the choppy gospel piano, we had sung to each other in enthusiastic nasal voices that "we were sinking deep in sin," but also that there is

> a fountain, filled with blood,
> drawn from Emmanuel's veins;
> and sinners plunged beneath that flood
> lose all their guilty stains.

"There is none righteous, no, not one," the deacon would have read from his worn, red-letter King James Bible, its spine crumbling in his hands.

Even John Bundy, my pear-shaped great-uncle who still lived at home with my great-grandparents, would have had a part in reminding us of what we couldn't forget. Having changed out of his striped blue overalls and smelly work boots, he would be dressed in a pair of round-toed black shoes and shiny gray pants barely held onto his belly by a slippery looking belt. "Oh, Lord," he would pray, bowing his head and scrunching up his creased and sweating brown face, "you *know* we are all sinners who *deserve* to *die,* but you *love* us and you sent *Jesus,* your *son,* to die a *terrible* death for us instead."

As a child I loved to go to revivals with my great-aunts, at the same time that the revivals terrified me. The talk about sin and rottenness and the rage of God the Father made sense. I was always aware there was something fatally wrong with me. As the smallest child I had figured out that there must be very few acceptable people in the world. In Sturgis a large portion of family conversation was spent deploring the existence of people who weren't part of our family—particularly, it seemed to me, women who didn't know "how to do," who didn't work till they dropped, or have widely admired children. "The only reason this family ever accepted me," Uncle Quentin's wife, Aunt Hilda, once told me, "is because somebody figured out I was a distant cousin." At home in New York my daddy ridiculed everybody I knew: women first, but also police, schoolteachers, Nash owners, Brooklynites, Yankees fans, Catholics, Jews, Protestants, his mother and sister, do-gooders, my friends, and my mother's friends.

All this ridicule of people I wanted to be allowed to like and respect told me that if none of these other people could measure up as human beings, I could never measure up either. If I already irritated my earthly father daily, I could certainly never meet the far stricter standards of my heavenly Father. I was bad through and through. I got in trouble in school for not finishing my work. I was a girl. I lied. I was always angry with my parents, and the very word *obey* made me feel sullen and resentful. I wanted to read instead of helping Mama. I imagined kissing Larry from across the apartment complex. I wouldn't hold still and stand on both feet when Mama hemmed my skirts, I had nightmares, I was afraid of everything, and I was unhappy.

Under the circumstances, the language of sin gave me a way to explain myself to myself. It told me what was wrong with me, why I felt as though I stood perpetually under the judgment of the whole universe. As a child, the meaning of "sin" was relatively straightforward. My very being was so sinful that God himself was enraged.

Revival talk about the sacrifice of Jesus was tougher to understand. *Sacrifice,* unlike *sin,* was a difficult-to-live-with, many-layered word I heard outside of church as well as inside. As a nine-year-old, I would have been hard pressed to say precisely what it meant if I had been asked its range of meanings, but I would have recognized them all if someone could have defined them for me. Sacrifice, after all, was the stuff of my life, of all of our lives.

In the aftermath of the Great Depression and the Second World War, to the child I was, the most obvious meaning of sacrifice had nothing to do with shed blood. It was about "doing without." It meant that, rather than spending my allowance for what I wanted in the present, I should save my money for some indefinite future. "Sacrificing" was doing without what you wanted just because it was good to do without what you wanted. Children should "learn to sacrifice." Modern children "had too much," my father proclaimed every Christmas Eve as I wondered guiltily about the next day's presents. Though no one had ever said so in so many words, it was clear to me that the ultimate goal of "learning to sacrifice" was to learn not to want anything at all.

Church talk about God's demand for sacrifice complemented this primary meaning in a horrible sort of way, as the attempted sacrifice of Isaac illustrated. The story went like this. A long time ago there was an old man named Abraham who didn't have any children. One day, God told Abraham that he was going to send his wife, Sarah, a little boy. When Isaac, the son, was born, Abraham loved him more than anything in the world. God didn't like this, so one day God decided to test Abraham. "Abraham," God said to him, "I don't want you to love anybody or anything as much as me. If you love me, you will have to prove it to me by sacrificing Isaac on the mountain I will show you. I don't mean that I want you to dedicate him to me. I want you to kill him. Have you got that?" "Yes, Lord," Abraham said; and to prove how much he loved God, when he and Isaac went up the mountain, he even made Isaac carry the knife. In the end, God rescued Isaac, but the point had been made: God had demanded Isaac as a sacrifice just because Abraham had wanted him so much, and because Abraham was good, he had handed Isaac right over.

Sacrifice, therefore, in its most basic secular and sacred context, meant giving up what you most wanted and loved because it was bad to want anything a lot. In this sense, everybody was supposed to sacrifice. But over and above this, "sacrifice" also had a specialized, particular meaning that applied to women in family life. Real women were supposed to suffer on behalf of their husbands and children, and this suffering was called "sacrifice." If the mother was exhausted with a new baby and the baby cried in the night, it was mama who got up because daddy needed his sleep. If there were two pieces of chicken and three family members, mother smilingly went hungry. If there were three silver forks and one battered, black fork, that was the one mother took. In the forties and fifties this behavior was expected of all mothers, not just mine. A woman's sacrifices proved to her husband and children that she loved them, and to the world that she was a good woman. They were the foundation of her moral authority in her family; without them she could never hope to win the guilty gratitude of her children and her husband.

Because everyone saw these sacrifices as a necessary part of being wife and mother, they were not necessarily a free expression of love. I was nine years old when I first learned that a good, sacrificing woman was expected to give up more than simply her desires, her needs, or even her lifeblood. A sacrificing woman was to be "selfless," and this selflessness included bearing the consequences of the sins of her husband and children. I first began to realize this, I remember, one late afternoon when my mother was in the early stages of pregnancy with my brother Wesley.

On that late, bleak winter day all the curlered mothers of Oakland Gardens were cooking supper and vacuuming for the homecoming of the fathers. A woman whose name I can't recall came from across the courtyard to summon my mother to the stoop in front of the apartment. Several other mothers were already huddled there, shivering with their hands in their pockets or their arms crossed on their chests.

In the confusion, I was able to sneak down the stairs behind my mother and hide within earshot.

"What is it?" somebody in a blue housedress asked. "What's going on?"

"It's Carol," someone in a maroon chenille bathrobe answered. The sound of her voice told me something had happened.

Carol was Mrs. McInerny. She, her husband, and her two children lived in a second-floor apartment just like ours around the keyhole from our part of the complex. I had been to their apartment for coffee cake after school with my mama and some other mothers not very long ago. I liked Mrs. McInerny. She had been nice to me. She had sat down on the floor with me and asked me questions about myself as though she had liked me. To my mind, she was an exotic woman of substance, a nurse, who had later given her baby a shot in her own kitchen right there in front of me. Nevertheless, I had also noticed her worn brown sweater covered with nits and pulls, her pale skin and wispy hair, and the dirty mustard furniture, the drab beige rug, and the drawn shades.

"What!" "What is it?" "What, what!" the mothers cried.

The nameless woman spoke. "You won't believe it. I was just talking to Betty, her downstairs neighbor. You know what Betty said? She said that when Jimmy came home from Scouts yesterday, he walked into the bedroom and found his mother hanging from the ceiling with a note to Bob pinned to her dress. Can you imagine!"

I stopped breathing. What had happened to Mrs. McInerny? My chest hurt and my mouth went dry in excruciating sympathy. I imagined I could hear her crying, and feel her fear and loneliness, her desperation and despair during her last few minutes of her life as she wrote her note and fastened it to her hem.

Then the angry voices of the adult conversation faded back in. " . . . Selfish! That's what she was, just selfish!" the women's voices went on. "She was only thinking about herself! We all know that man was running around on her, but that's what men do. What was wrong with her, anyway? She should have been willing to sacrifice!"

Now I was truly paralyzed with horror. Mrs. McInerny was dead, and not one grown-up said she was sorry or wondered out loud about what she had felt. Were those women mostly worried about the poor little boy who had found his mother? I don't know, but at the time it seemed to me that the mothers were angry because by dying Mrs. McInerny had refused to be a real woman.

But, apart from love of her children, why should Mrs. McInerny have accepted this burden of blame and punishment? This gets us to the other side of what I as a child understood the reason for such an expectation of self-sacrifice to be. As a little girl, I do not recall being told much about the original sin of Eve, but I do remember connecting the need for women's sacrifices with their culpable inferiority to men. It seemed to me that those wives and mothers must have expected Mrs. McInerny to bear the brunt of her husband's infidelity simply because she was a woman in the first place. Women suffered what men did not have to suffer because they deserved to suffer for being only women. This was the obvious explanation of why women had to do what their husbands told them. It was also why, unlike my brothers, when I became a grown-up I could never be president. Women could never become artists or writers or business people or scientists or intellectuals or even ministers. It wasn't that we weren't allowed to do these things so much as we weren't able, and so for this sin of inability we paid the price: we sacrificed ourselves.

As complicated as the general and specialized meanings of "sacrifice" were, trying to understand the sacrifice of Jesus in the context of these meanings was hard work. To begin, though I don't remember consciously pondering it, I must have thought in those very early years that if sacrifice is the law of human life, it must be the divine law as well. If it is good for human beings to give up what they want simply because they want it, it must be good for God, too. "God so loved the world that he sent his only son. . . ." Abraham was willing to kill his son, and even God the Father, in the same spirit, must have sent his own son for the express purpose of being killed as well.

At the same time, Pond Fork Baptist Church had made it very clear to me that God's giving up Jesus was not quite in the same category as a mother getting up in the night with the baby so that the daddy could sleep. Sin was the fundamental cause of all human suffering, and Jesus bore the brunt of it just as surely as wives were supposed to bear the brunt of their husband's and children's sins. My sin—my lying, my being unhappy, my disobedience, my femaleness—all these were the actual cause of Jesus' sacrifice.

But past this point, how did it all hang together? Sometimes what I heard at church suggested that the Father's sacrifice of Jesus had something to do with God's need to provide the death of his only son to pay off some unspeakable debt I had run up without intend-

ing it. I wasn't actually very clear about the nature of
this debt. I knew, however, that God had made Jesus
come to earth for the express purpose of paying it,
though I wasn't sure for what or to whom it was to be
paid. Sometimes it was God's "justice" that demanded
it; sometimes it was the devil. I couldn't tell the difference; I was terrified of the unlimited anger and power
of God and the devil, both. One of my most frightening
childhood dreams featured me strapped into a dentist's
chair in a darkened church basement, my eyes fixed
feverishly on a neon cross on the wall while the devil
danced around me, dental instruments in hand.

A simpler, logically vague, but emotionally convinc-
ing explanation left out the debt and the devil altogether
and revolved instead around the ever-present anger of
God the Father. My human father, God knew, loved me
very much but he was also angered easily by his daughter's sins, particularly the sin of disobedience, for which
there were never an escape from punishment. The worst
part of punishment was never the spanking, but my
father's insistence that I acknowledge my absolute
wrongness and his absolute rightness. Stubborn and
easily humiliated child that I was, this felt to me like
death.

Everything I had heard in church told me that my
heavenly Father was a parent even stricter than mine.
As a parent, he loved us very much, but in the matter of
his power and authority, his anger was more danger-

ously volatile than that of my human father. Although God loved us, by our sin we had enraged God so much that punishment wasn't enough. Somebody had to die for it. Jesus was that somebody.

But did God in this sense kill Jesus, or did Jesus choose it? Whatever else I believed as a nine-year-old about the crucifixion, I didn't believe that Jesus was simply killed against his will. Obedient to the Father even unto death, Jesus had chosen his death in exactly the same ways and for the same three reasons women sacrificed themselves for their husbands and children. First, he had to prove to us that he loved us by pouring over us fountains of his blood. Second, he had to show us he was so good that he had wanted nothing for himself, not even his own life. Third, he accepted it as his role in life to bear the brunt of what we had done wrong. And there was a fourth reason as well. Jesus wanted us to know without a shadow of doubt that all Christians, but especially Christian women, were to sacrifice themselves exactly like him.

There was a small problem in this understanding of the work of Christ. Unlike women, the obligation on Jesus to sacrifice himself did not follow upon his being female. After all, as a human being, Jesus was perfect, free of sin, and male. This difficulty was removed for me at the time, however, by the way I understood Jesus' subordinate place with respect to God the Father. The Father was to Jesus as husband was to wife.

This was the way in which the inner logic of the crucifixion as it was governed by the notion of sin, sacrifice, and love attracted, terrified, and repelled the nine-year-old me. After my parents were divorced when I was eleven and a half, my mother was left with very few resources, and the care of my little brothers and me. It was only as I lived with and loved my mother in the years that followed that I came to experience another and far more painful dimension to the meaning of the crucifixion as I understood it then and its inner relationship to love, sin, and sacrifice.

The years of my adolescence were difficult years for us all, but they were made unbearable to me by my awareness of the special hardship of my mother's life. Not only did she wrestle daily with her own devouring grief and anger; as a proud woman for whom the care of her family had always been primary, she had to suffer the fear and judgmentalism of the fifties toward divorced women. But this was only part of it. Without an education and no job experience since her marriage thirteen years earlier, she was also left at the mercy of a world that wouldn't pay her a living wage for her "women's work" as a secretary. Later, when I turned fifteen and was allowed to work at Grant's, I learned that, as hard as Mama's life was, it was not nearly as hard as the lives of many other women with children or elderly parents to support on their solitary salaries. My work at Grant's was the end of my belief that there was something natural and right about the sacrifices women bore in their families and in the larger society as well.

My brother Fred learned the same lesson directly from my mother when he was about sixteen and she had told him to get out of bed and do some yard work.

"I can't get up and mow the grass for you," he had answered, one summer Saturday morning about eleven o'clock. "I'm too tired."

"How do you think I feel?" my irritated mother replied.

"That's different," said Fred, with all the complacency a teen-aged male of the fifties could muster. "You're a mother. You're tough. You can take it."

"Get out there and mow," she answered, yanking him out of bed in his undershorts, "and don't you dare say anything like that again!"

The fact was that, however much worse off many women were, what I knew was that Mother's life was hard in a way it never would have been if she had not had us children. It was because of us that she had to work so hard. It was our laundry she wore herself out doing, our bills she had to pay. It was our meals she stood at the stove and cooked in the hot summer evenings when she got home from work. It was to pay for my flute lessons that she did without things herself. It was because of us she had almost no time or energy for friends. In sum, it was for our well-being alone that she had sacrificed and would continue to sacrifice everything of her own wants and needs.

In the face of all my mother's sacrifices I was full only of an overwhelming sense of unworthiness and obligation I could never meet. I could not bear to feel my mother's suffering. I was the cause of her hurt. I ought to be able to make it up to her by being who she wanted me to be, but I couldn't. I still hadn't learned not to want things, and now, when we had no money, it really mattered. My grades were low; I was lazy; I was shy; I never wrote my thank-you notes; I was even more afraid of my father than I had been as a child, even less like the people my parents and my parents' families seemed to admire. Worst of all my sins, I was more unhappy than ever.

I knew I was unworthy of my mother's sacrifices, and the shame and guilt that I carried because of what she was suffering on behalf of my sorry self left me helpless. The whole situation filled me day and night with sullen rage. I did not want to be sacrificed for; I did not want my life in the place of my mother's. I did not want my mother's loneliness and anxiety and exhaustion. And most of all I did not want the whole burden of the pressure to be worthy of all my mother's love and pain.

My poor mother! Any attempts to tell Mama how I felt always ended up in the same place. I could never explain myself in a way that made sense to her. "I can't understand how you feel," she would say, baffled and beside herself with frustration over unjust accusations she couldn't even understand. "You are just fine the way you are. I don't care about your grades. You children are all I've got! Just grow up to be good people. All I want is for you to be happy." The only thing she wanted I could not give her. All those sacrifices for nothing.

How could I ever get out from under the burden of all this sacrifice and love and unworthiness? Recognizing in my life the familiar themes of Pond Fork's summer revivals, over the spring and summer of my freshman year of high school I made friends with two kind-hearted evangelical fellow students. Though neither of them believed in Brother Smith's angry and vengeful God, they had no idea how to understand my unhappiness except in the familiar terms of sin and repentance.

"I feel so bad," I told my friends, tears running down my cheeks, sitting on a gray rock at Good News Camp.

" 'There is none righteous, no not one,' " Douglas answered me, and I marked it in on the India paper of my beautiful, thin red Bible he had given me.

"You feel bad because you are a sinner," Jane Anne said, gently. I knew this was true.

"God cannot tolerate sin, but God loves you and sent Jesus to die for your sins." When they added, "Repent and believe the Good News that God loves you enough for Christ to die for you and accept Jesus as your personal Lord and Savior," I was in trouble. The trouble wasn't in the repenting part. I had been repenting of everything I was with my whole heart as long as I could remember; now, I was only stepping up my efforts.

The trouble was in the business about sacrifice. My mother was sacrificing for me every day. She hadn't literally died, and I couldn't stand it. Now I was being told that because of my sin, Jesus had actually gone through with it and died. How on earth could this be good news? I could never survive that cosmic burden of guilt and gratitude and obligation. No matter how many prayer meetings I went to, no matter how much I repented or how many times I asked Jesus to come into my life as my personal Lord and Savior, it never worked; I just couldn't believe.

It was soon after this failed experiment that I fell in love with my high school boyfriend and his Unitarian family. During the rest of my high school years in the shadow of their rational humanism I had some superficial relief from the burden of Jesus' sacrifice. Still, the facts of sin, love, and sacrifice were not so easy to escape as all that.

The end of my childhood coincided with my marriage at eighteen to another boy whom I wanted to marry, I think now, not just because he reminded me of my father, but because at some dim level he also seemed to offer me a way out from under the burden of my unworthiness of my mother's love and sacrifices. He believed entirely in what I had learned as a child about the importance of sacrifice for women. Wives sacrifice; husbands receive. If I could prove my love to him by the sacrifices I could make; if I could become the one sacrificing rather than the one sacrificed for, I would no longer be unworthy. I would be an adult woman. I would be free. My sacrifices would quench my burning anger and my raging guilt.

Of course, none of it worked out as I had thought it should, and the time of that marriage was very hard. At the same time much good took place in those years. I finished college and I spent two years in seminary. I did my graduate work at Oxford University in England, in Hebrew, then in early church history. It was during this time in the Bodleian Library that I first met the generous and gentle God of the early monks through the sixth-century monophysite bishop, Philoxenus of Mabbug.

It was also then in the great library of Oxford that I first read more widely in the ancient theology of early Eastern Christian writers such as Athanasius and Gregory of Nyssa, and from them my heart began to receive hints of a new way of thinking about the crucifixion of Jesus Christ.

In the beginning, Athanasius told me,[1] God created all things and declared them good. Human beings, however, were particularly good because they were created in God's own image and given the gift of rationality in order to enable them to see God in the world around them, and thus to know and love God. To enable this knowing and loving and to prevent them from dying like all the other creatures God had made, they were placed in the Garden of Eden and given the special gift of immortality.

All, however, did not remain well. Through the disobedience of Adam and Eve humanity left the Garden with the image of God badly damaged. Two interlocking consequences for the rest of us human beings followed. First, from that time forward human lives increasingly became dominated by death and the fear of death. Second, with our reason no longer working properly, our ability to see and know God in the world and in one another was seriously impaired. Thus, living in a self-invented world of our own blind, obsessive emotions, needs, fears, and desires, we increasingly hurt ourselves and others as we lost our ability to love.

Because God loved us and intended our well-being, God would not leave us in our wounded state of sin. God sent both the laws and the prophets for our healing,

---

1. *St. Athanasius: On the Incarnation of God the Word,* par. 1-34 (Crestwood, N.Y.: St. Vladimir's Press, 1953).

but neither was effective, for we still could not see reality. Then, at last, when all else had failed, God the Word, in God's own person, as God and as a human being, came among us to bring us healing, to restore to us the image of God, to uncloud our vision, to destroy the power of death, and to teach us once again the way to love.

None of this had much to do with my childhood vision of the cross dominated by images of a father God angry over my sin, and a son who, to prove his love, paid for it in my place by sacrificing himself. It was equally far from my adolescent understanding of Jesus, selflessly suffering for the hopelessly unworthy.

Indeed, in the equation "sin + love + sacrifice = salvation" the early church redefined all the terms. They did not see sin as our hopeless badness. Sin was about being blinded and wounded by our own and society's patterns of seeing, feeling, and acting so that we could not love one another or God. God did not love us sternly in spite of our unworthiness, nor was God or Jesus victimized by God's love. In fact, God was not even interested in questions of worthiness or unworthiness. For some inexplicable reason, God actually liked us, and Jesus suffered not because suffering in itself is a necessary proof of love. Rather, Jesus chose to suffer in order that the hold death had on us would be loosened and the image of God be restored in us so that we could once again learn how to love.

How good all this sounded! I lay awake night after night in the beautiful Oxford silence pondering all the gifts it would bring me if I could really believe what I was reading. In the end, I couldn't let myself believe, because to give up the older images of God and love, sacrifice and sin that it would replace would mean admitting that almost everything in my life was wrong. This included not just my relationship with God, but the very shape of my relationships with my husband, my father, my mother, and especially with myself. Even so, whether I chose it or not, the seed of the early church had been planted within me.

After three years in England, I returned to the States. I gave birth to a daughter and I began to teach college. I completed my dissertation, and I gave birth to a son. All this time, nourished by my research, my pondering, and the mysterious gift of God's grace, the seed grew and made its own space. Increasingly, it became impossible for me to live my married life under the ever growing weight of the old images of sin, sacrifice, and love. Nine years after we left England, my husband and I separated and divorced.

The next year I came to teach in Atlanta, and as the plant the seed had become began to bear very small but real fruit, all the old categories of sin, sacrifice, and love promised to be gone. At the end of that first year, half-crazed and laughing with love, I married Richard, a curly-haired, green-eyed, gentle man who knew how to enjoy life.

Richard was an old friend and student, and I had fallen in love with him one day when I had invited him back to the house after I had run into him in the grocery store. The children were little, and that long, hot day had already been too much for me. Coming in the door with Richard behind me, I had flung myself down at the kitchen table. I remember saying, "I am so thirsty," and the next thing I remember after that is that Richard got up from his chair without a word and took down a glass from the cupboard. Then he got ice cubes from the refrigerator, added water from the tap, and brought me the glass of water. In my astonishment that a man would ever do such a thing for me I had fallen in love, and this was the man I was now married to. Richard not only loved me; he liked me. He not only wanted to share in all the household work of our marriage, he actually wanted to do things for me over and above that. He did not expect me to prove my love to him by what I was willing to give up or accept for him. He could not even understand the idea of suffering and sacrifice and unworthiness upon which my former life had been based.

During those first years of our marriage I was very literally hardly able to believe my good fortune. Half of my unbelief had to do with who Richard was himself, but the other half was caused by that old configuration of love, sacrifice, and my sense of myself as unworthy of the sacrifice Richard must be making by loving me. I was consumed by anxiety that I would lose Richard. My fears were equally divided between worry that he would come to his senses, see me for who I was and leave me, and worry that he would get sick, have an accident—or, as my dream told me, decide to die in my place for my sins. It was at the end of those first three years that I had the dream of murder in the green-tiled bathroom.

The dream, as I knew even at the time, had been a gift of grace to help me out of the old world of my childhood and early adulthood and into the new world I had first glimpsed in my graduate school years. Over the next three years or so as I struggled with my anxieties and fears about Richard, I worked both in my prayer and out to unravel the meaning of my dream with respect both to my marriage and to the meaning of the crucifixion. In the end, even *my* heart was mostly convinced that the old way of understanding the links between love and sacrifice and sin was dead wrong. I no longer felt like an amnesiac stroke victim as I continued to teach the christology of the early church. But what *was* the meaning of the crucifixion for me? On that point I still dwelt entirely in the darkness.

It was three years after my dream that the meaning of the crucifixion began to become clear. It started with a Palm Sunday service on an ordinary gray spring day in Cannon Chapel. As usual, our family was running late, and I was distracted throughout the start of worship. Then, we came to a dramatic reading of Mark's Passion narrative, and I found myself wholly attentive. With no effort on my part, I had gone from hearing the story as an outside observer to experiencing myself as present in the events that were being narrated as if I were someone who had known and loved Jesus personally for a long time. As I heard the reading, I watched him move through the shouting crowds on the day of palms. I heard his anguish in the garden, and I sneaked along behind the soldiers after his arrest. When at last, by the fire in the courtyard, even Peter abandoned him, angrily insisting in Jesus' hearing that he didn't even know Jesus, I couldn't take it anymore. I heard nothing after that. I left church grieving, angry at God, and totally uninterested in whatever good reasons God might have had for what was about to happen to this good man I loved so much.

The scene of betrayal by the flickering fire was still oddly alive in my mind as I stumbled through the rest of the day with my family. The next morning I awoke to an experience even odder than that of the day before. As I dressed myself, got the children off to school, went to school myself and participated in our Monday meetings, I experienced myself standing in the yellow dust of Golgotha at the very foot of the cross, and I was no longer an anonymous observer as I had been the day before. Now I stood by Jesus as his mother.

Under a blazing sun, as close as I was allowed to be, I stood there, feeling the heat radiating from the legs of this man who was my child, and my heart was breaking. All I could remember was the baby he had been, his sweetness, his arms around my neck, his nursing mouth. What I had wanted as his mother was to love him and keep him safe, and now I could not. What did I care what God's reasons were? I was not interested in explanations of sin or love or anything else. There could be no reasons for this death that were good enough for me.

As Mary, I lived through two more days of the crucifixion that week at the same time I continued to go about my everyday life. By Wednesday afternoon the vivid images and the piercing grief had faded, and I was left tired, confused, and once again entirely in my own world. I didn't know whether something terrible had happened to me or if I had been given some great gift. I think by then I hated God. As far as I was concerned, it was over. Mothers have no interest in divine explanations of the deaths of their children.

The next two days were a fog of pain and anger. Then, on Good Friday evening, I went reluctantly to church again with my family to hear the biblical account of the crucifixion. This time as I heard the familiar readings I felt drained, and the readings sounded flat. Then, we arrived at the end of the story and I heard Jesus' last words, and I was once again drawn into what I was hearing, and once again my perspective leaped. Now, as Jesus spoke those dreadful words "My God, my God, why have you forsaken me?" I no longer heard them filtered through the pain of Jesus' human mother. Now I was hearing them from within the truly unendurable pain and yearning love of God, his heavenly mother.

Suddenly, the meaning of the Gospel narratives, Jesus' actions and his teaching, presented itself clearly to me in a way it never had before. God had never wanted, and certainly never needed, Jesus' death. Jesus himself was no passively obedient, selflessly suffering deflector of God's wrath at human imperfection. Jesus was no subordinate of God, mindlessly doing God's will in submissively loving obedience. It was Jesus who had made the choices leading to the cross.

As for God's part in the crucifixion, in that moment I couldn't imagine how I could ever have been taken in by a picture of an all-powerful, angry parent God whose love somehow demanded the blood-payment of God's own child for the sins and imperfections of the world. In the story of the prodigal son[2] Jesus himself tells a story about what God is like as a father, and as a mother, too. The story of the prodigal son is not about judgment. What does that father of the prodigal care for his son's wrongdoing? The character of the father in the story expresses itself in the willingness of his love to let his children make their own decisions about their lives, even to the point of losing them. The pain of his love is terrible as he stands there every day on his front porch,

---

2. Luke 15.

squinting down the road into the sun for an unlikely glimpse of the child he loves.

For parents who would never abandon their lost or wounded or dying children, for mothers and fathers who yearn to comfort and protect their daughters and sons and keep them safe, there can be no more awful words to hear than: "Mama, Daddy, my God, why have you forsaken me?" And, because out of love, God did not intervene at the cross, but let Jesus choose his own way, these were the words God heard.

As for Jesus, himself, what had Jesus chosen? Certainly not a love that requires suffering as its proof; certainly not death to pay the price for anybody's real or imagined sins. In that moment in church on Good Friday, I was able to know for the first time that, though I had sinned and sinned again, my fundamental problem was not caused by a need to repent. Hardly any of my misery from childhood on had come from my own badness; it had come from my shame at not living up to harmful yet typical family standards, shame at being female in a world that curled its lip at women, and shame over my unworthiness of the sacrifices that had characterized my mother's life as a divorced woman with children.

How could I repent of the things that had happened to me without me choosing them, of having been made a woman, of my very being? I did not need to repent. I needed to be rescued from my shame. And this is what I now could see was exactly what Jesus as the privileged one of God, as God's own self, had chosen to do by casting in his lot not only with me but with all women and men the world would shame and reduce to nothing for simply being who they are.

And not only to the inconspicuously shamed like me and those like me, but also to the raped woman, blamed for the rape, to the divorced woman trying to support her children on a secretary's salary while her church preaches to her about "family values," to young people with blackened teeth because they can't afford the price of a dentist, to the uneducated and the ignorant, to the one with the "wrong" color skin who can't get a mortgage in his own neighborhood, to the day laborer who is treated as an animal by his employer, to the man with AIDS, to the man whose children have contempt for him because he can't find a job, to the "unmanly" man who weeps real tears, to the mentally ill old woman living in a pile of newspapers on Social Security disability, to the man who is ridiculed by his friends when they learn that he gets up in the night with his baby so that his wife may sleep, to all of these Jesus speaks:

"Do not be ashamed. I cast in my lot with you, as God and as a human being. From the time I heard the cry of the despised slaves in Egypt, I have sought to rescue you who are shamed. Yes, you have sinned, and you have repented in abundance, but it is the *world* that is the source of your shame, not your own sin.

"It is your suffering shame that consumes you with anger, that renders you passive, that swallows you in depression, that keeps you from loving and knowing yourself to be loved. You do not bear your shame as the rightful price you pay for some imagined unworthiness.

"A bruised reed, I will not break you; a smoldering wick, I will never quench you.[3] I hate the shame that binds you and destroys you, and I will prove it to you and to the world by casting in my lot with you even so far as to die a death the world finds shameful. By showing you the source and meaning of your shame, I will make a space for you to breathe and thrive. This is what I, Jesus, as a human being in the image of God, and as God's own self, chose with great joy."

Easter that year was different from what it had been any other year. Though I had much work left to do, the cross, God, Jesus, sacrifice, love, sin, my own history—none would ever be the same for me. I knew now for myself that the early church had been right. In God's active presence in Jesus' gift on and at the cross lay the possibility for the healing of our wounds, the restoring of vision, and our ability to love.

---

3. Isaiah 42:3.

Resurrection

I always knew that the crucifixion was important, complex, about me as well as about Jesus. Even during the years when its meaning was entirely opaque to me, I could not simply let the crucifixion go without trying to understand it because I was sure my life somehow depended on it. The resurrection was another matter. It was simple and embarrassing, about Jesus and not about me. The idea of resurrection was so alien to me that, after some childhood experimentation to discover whether I could make myself believe that a dead body could come to life again, I hardly ever gave it a thought until five years ago, the spring of my forty-seventh year.

When I was a little child, I longed to be good, or rather, I longed for all the grown-ups I loved to smile at me together and say, "Well done, thou good and faithful servant." During the years before I started school, when my parents and I lived with my aunt and my father's mother in Flushing, New York, there was small chance of that.

In one of my earliest memories I am standing on a tall chair in front of a mirror admiring my curly-haired reflection. Though the room itself is dark, the sun is bright outside. I know that my mother is out some-where, and my grandmother, who stands beside me with scissors in her hand, is telling me how beautiful I am about to be. What a nice surprise it is going to be for my mother, she says, and how pleased she is going to be with me when she sees me! I am delighted. I stand very still, as I feel the cold points of the scissors scrape gently across the skin of my forehead, and I do not wiggle at all as my hair tickles my nose falling down the front of my light green dress my mother has made me. My grandmother is finished. She brushes me off and spits on her fingers. She pinches my hair to make my new bangs curl. She stands back to look at me, then she squeezes me. "Just wait till your mother gets home," she says. I put my arms around her neck. I am happy. My grandmother is pleased with me. I am good.

The events that followed my mother's return are not so clear in my mind. I remember Mama's tense voice, though I have no memory of what she said to my grandmother—surely something like, "How could you have cut my baby's hair without even asking me?" I remember Mama's rage at my grandmother. I was afraid. I knew I had been bad because my mother was mad at me, and I had made her cry. I wasn't sure what it was I had done, but I had learned something significant: being good is not always a straightforward, easy matter. By doing what it took to be good in my grandmother's eyes, I had to be bad in my mother's.

Though it happened, I can hardly imagine my mother living in my grandmother's house. Nanaw was an unusually strong and admirable woman in her time. She was the fourth child of German immigrant parents who had already lost a boy and a girl, and when polio at two crippled her, her aristocratic mother rejected her, saying, "God always takes the good ones." Perhaps it was because she had to fight so hard for her own survival that Nanaw ran over everybody. A liberal Democrat and a progressive Presbyterian, she spoke her mind on every subject at all times, appropriately or not, and she was utterly convinced of her own superiority and that of the rest of her blood kin in all things that mattered. Her marriage to my grandfather Joe was miserable. Joe, a crime reporter for every major newspaper in Manhattan at one time or another, was no prize package as a husband, and they were divorced around the time when I was born. My grandmother was not very domestic.

Though she had no formal education, she supported herself right up till she retired with a series of jobs like the one she had when we lived with her; she was then the director of a home for the mentally ill. My grandmother expected nothing of me she wasn't already getting: she thought everything I did was perfect, and I loved to hear her say, "Roberta is so smart; she takes after her father!"

My grandmother drove my mother crazy all her life. Mother grew up in Western Kentucky in a farm family every bit as convinced of its superiority as Nanaw was of her family's. As much as Mama might have agreed with Nanaw on some subjects (and there weren't many), the very way my grandmother went about expressing a certain opinion was enough to turn Mama against it. The women in mother's family were smart and educated, but they believed it was crude to argue about politics, talk about religion outside of church, or feminine hygiene at the dinner table in front of men and children, and they believed that only fools got excited about social causes. My mother's mother, my great-grandmother, my great-aunts and aunts in those days worked hard, and city women like Nanaw who slept till seven o'clock and didn't do the kind of work they valued were at best ridiculous and at worst contemptible. The Wynn and Wesley women looked for a lot from their daughters in the way of the solid accomplishments of a farm woman's life, and good moral character, and they got what they expected. Mama expected the same of me. At the same time, Mama wanted me to be the daughter who would do her proud before her mother-in-law and husband. She hated the excuses my grandmother made for me when I did something bad, and her back would go straight and stiff when my grandmother praised me. "I only want you to be good," she would say to me. "I only want you to do the right thing."

My father was the third sun in my one-planet solar system. Self-educated, with a photographic memory and voracious curiosity about absolutely everything, he was, indeed, as my grandmother would say, "smart." He was good looking, funny, affectionate, and charming to women, including his daughter. Unlimited in his own energy, he was always building something—furniture, phonographs, or racing cars. Like my grandmother, he was convinced of his own superiority, especially as a sophisticated Manhattanite, but unlike his mother he ridiculed religion, priests, and ministers; he detested politicians and government in all its forms, as well as communists, the police, schoolteachers, and above all, women. He loved my mother very much, though he saw her as his subordinate whose successes and rare failures as a housewife reflected directly on him. As for me, his daughter, his expectations were very high. I was to be quiet, obedient, and domestic. At the same time, impossibly, I was to be, like him, smart, creative, and independent of the opinions of "others."

How I loved these three in the years before I started school, and how much I wanted to do the things that pleased them all, to be good for them all! I wanted to act the way they explicitly told me they wanted me to act and be the child they told me they wanted me to be. There was never a chance. It was not only that on the battleground of the undeclared war among the grown-ups, I never could have succeeded. Even individually, my mother and father had so many things they wanted for me that conflicted with each other.

As a child, however, I could never see the impossibility of fulfilling all the self-contradictory things they wanted. Instead, I tried all the harder. It seemed to me that the trouble must lie in my having missed something, so I threw myself into pleasing them, trying to be good by learning to listen for and seek out their most secret, unspoken criticisms and expectations.

I think it was when I started kindergarten, long after we moved out of my grandmother's house, about the time when I got good at figuring out what I thought Mama and Daddy really wanted of me, that I learned that there was no way I could be good. I could not defend myself in school if someone picked on me and be obedient to the teacher who told us never to fight. I could not figure out how to combine my father's words, "Those who can, do, those who can't, teach," with, "You respect your teacher, and do what she says, or you will answer to me." I could not be ever watchful of what the neighbors would think at the same time that I was not to care if everybody else was allowed to do something and I wasn't. It never occurred to me that the problem was not in me. I only knew that whatever I did right, it made me wrong about something else. This, I believe, was the beginning of the depression that pressed me down until I was over forty-five years old.

In early grade school, as at home, "being good" was not so much about morals as it was about earning the teacher's approval, an almost impossible goal under the circumstances. In those days in Queens the schools were terribly overcrowded. There were more than forty children in my second-grade classroom. Miss Stillwell, who was young and stylish in a hard sort of way, was not good at distinguishing one child from another, and some of the children dealt with their anonymity more aggressively than others. Once, I recall, five or six boys in the class played a trick on her. I can still see them pointing to her leg as they stretched forward over their battered wooden desks, faces plastered over with malicious grins, shouting that she had a run in her stocking. I remember, too, both the undiscriminating quality of her bitter anger, and my bewildered sense of guilt, fear, and helpless responsibility for the punishment of the whole class that followed.

By the time I was in the fourth grade I was in serious trouble in school. I had no interest in learning or doing anything because it was interesting to me or important in itself. My anxiety to please and my self-consciousness made me unable to concentrate. I could not learn the multiplication tables and long division and spelling. I couldn't make myself do my homework, and I didn't finish class assignments. I got bad grades. I was unhappy, and that in itself angered and frustrated my teachers.

At home I was no better. There, too, I had a hard time following simple directions or completing tasks. I forgot to ask for money for my school projects, and I couldn't make myself do my chores. I lost everything I got my hands on from sweaters and umbrellas to jewelry, and I couldn't find things other people sent me to look for. My father's solution to what he was sure was my laziness and carelessness was to get ever stricter, more disapproving, and more authoritarian. "Your teacher says you are an underachiever," he would proclaim in a voice that would have frightened an entire gang of juvenile delinquents. "We'll see about that. There won't be any desserts for you until you straighten up. No more privileges without responsibilities. Now straighten up, and quit crying or I'll give you something to cry about!"

Straighten up! I could no more have straightened up by myself than the bent-over woman whom Jesus healed in Luke 13. I knew very well that the grown-ups' accusations of laziness, carelessness, disobedience, and unhappiness were true. I loved my parents, and I was humiliated, deeply shamed by who I was for them. I looked in the mirror at my plain brown pigtails, my glasses, and my skinny body, and I hated myself. If I made them angry, then I embraced with a vengeance the task of doing their job for them when they weren't around. Daily, I recounted my failures to myself with the faithful and imaginative regularity of a praying saint. Making myself feel terrible was the one responsibility I could fulfill, willingly.

In the "badness" of my childhood depression, I was teeth-rattlingly lonely. I remember as a ten-year-old looking at a rock in the yard and starting to cry as I suddenly imagined myself as that rock, alone and silent forever. A version of this fantasy persisted even into seminary. What horror I felt when I learned that Origen believed that the sun and stars are really angels, singing praises to God for eternity! In my imagination I could not escape the loneliness of those thinking, feeling beings, hanging in empty space, separated from all other beings not just by miles but by light-years.

The conservative Christianity of my childhood offered me no way out of my unhappiness. Rather, with its emphasis on sin, on the thorough badness of all people, and Jesus' death for it, it gave me an explanation for why I ought to be depressed. Sin was what religion was about. If you had asked me in the fourth grade, "Why was Jesus born?" I would have been glad to answer, "It was because of sin. Jesus was born in order to pay the price for our sin by suffering and dying on the cross." If you had pushed me about what it took to get our sins forgiven, I would have told you: "We have to repent of our sins." If you had pushed me a little further to ask, "And what does it mean to repent?" I would have said, "To feel really, really bad about what a sinful person you are." And if you had nudged a little one more time to ask, finally, "What does Jesus' resurrection have to do with any of this?" I would have looked at you blankly. "The resurrection doesn't have anything to do with sin and forgiveness," I would have thought, but because you were a grown-up, still I would have answered you politely: "The resurrection means Jesus rose from the grave on Easter morning. If you don't believe it happened, just like if you don't believe God loves you and forgives your sins, you can't go to heaven."

Certainly, I never connected the resurrection with what actually did get me through my childhood and my adolescence, too: the experience of beauty. Daily, the ordinary sight of a perfect shape in a rock, the light coming through a piece of colored glass, the secret sound of bells in a wind harp always had the power to comfort and soothe me. But sometimes, when I hurt so much I could hardly bear it, I would experience something through the medium of beauty that for a moment would simply annihilate my pain and longing and helplessness. Then, the sunlight coming through a glass of water, or a single note of my flute would flash out with a power that would flood me with fierce happiness.

From my earliest childhood I regarded these experiences with a holy reverence. I believed that in these rare moments of flashing joy I was being allowed to look through a kind of window into the actual, good, generous, and powerful heart of the universe itself, a heart that belonged to a hidden God who loved me, but who was also, oddly, totally impersonal. By the time I was twelve I also believed that these glimpses of reality carried with them a single moral obligation: as I was rescued by them if only for a moment from my own isolation and hurt, so I must be sensitive to the hurts of other people as well.

But this is not the way it normally was. In the years of my adolescence and young adulthood when my world expanded, my need to be found acceptable and my desire to be good grew both stronger and more complex. The loss of my father with my parents' divorce filled me with a kind of cosmic grief and guilt, and in the years that followed our move to Kentucky, my depression and helplessness grew.

A major factor in the worsening of my depression was my secret conviction that, by my failures to live up to my father's expectations, I had permanently harmed my mother. I was the cause both of the divorce and of all her unhappiness and financial hardship that followed it. Because I was responsible, I decided in some inarticulate way that I was the one who must fix it for her, or at least in some way make it up to her. How horrified my mother would have been if she had known this!

First, if she was unhappy, I would make it up to her by being as unhappy as she was. In this way I would both show her I was sorry and make amends. Any real woman, I already knew, proves her love by accepting the suffering of the ones she loves as her own. At the same time, I would accept my unhappiness as no more than the rightful punishment I bore for my failures. Second, I would make her happy again by becoming the good and successful daughter she wanted, to become for her the daughter who would vindicate her in the eyes of my father, my grandmother, and my mother's family as well. I would grit my teeth, gird up my loins, and become a housekeeper to the standard of my aunts, a writer of letters to my grandmothers, a successful career woman dependent on no man, a wife who never argued with her husband, a brilliant intellect like my father, and a self-sacrificial mother like her, herself.

Given the way I picked up other people's feelings, the first task I had set myself—accepting the addition of the weight of my mother's unhappiness to my own—I could not have helped accomplishing even if I had tried not to. Indeed, since childhood I had been unable not to read other people's feelings of pain, dislike, depression, or anger and take them on as my own, and this had always especially been true of my mother's feelings. The second task, becoming the vindicator of my mother by being perfect, was impossible. Given all this, it is hardly surprising that I was often so depressed that I could barely make it back and forth to school.

My life most often seemed, hatefully, to present its interpretation to me in religious categories I could not escape. At the time I was convinced that what had always prevented me from being able to be happy and "normal" was the grip the conservative Christianity of my childhood still had on me, with its emphasis on sin, guilt, and the cross. Except in the moments when I escaped into an alternate universe through my music, its perfectionistic, rejecting, all-seeing God still held me nearly helpless in his depressing grip. Yet even in shouldering all this unhappiness, I never consciously accepted it as a good thing. I fought for myself by trying my best to embrace instead the distant watchmaker god and the cool rationality of the contented liberal Christianity of my Unitarian friends, the Taylor family.

I graduated from high school still fighting, and still trying unsuccessfully to live up to what I believed were my mother's expectations. Then my universe began to proliferate suns when I married a graduate student in chemistry at the end of my freshman year. His liberal religious convictions seemingly coincided with mine. Unfortunately, however, meeting my mother's or father's expectations was nothing compared to meeting his.

What he wanted of me as a wife was so manifold and self-contradictory that a thousand wives working at once could never have met them. Yet somehow, in the glow of having at least accomplished the task of getting married, however badly I knew I disappointed my husband, I pulled myself together enough to make good grades, graduating from college with a high enough grade-point average to be able to decide to go on to seminary to study Hebrew.

It had been an easy decision to make. I had intended to do graduate work in Renaissance English. Because I wanted to work with some Renaissance interpretation of some Genesis stories, it had seemed to be a good idea during my last summer before beginning the graduate program that I study a little Hebrew. Hebrew! I remember still how, when I picked up the Hebrew Bible and read for the first time the opening words of Genesis chapter 1, the very letters on the page seemed to dance with little flames of joy. In that moment of intense happiness I knew I was face to face with the God who had not just created the world and found it good, but created and rejoiced in me as well. I did not connect the God I met that day with my childhood's secret God of beauty. I could see only that if I could come to know this God I encountered on the Hebrew page, I would no longer have to justify my existence to myself, or to work so hard at being found acceptable by the many suns in my lonely universe.

My instant abandonment of English in exchange for Hebrew was, certainly, the first conscious step I took away from the unreal, perfectionistic God of my childhood toward the real God of life. The choice of Hebrew was also the first deliberate step I took that would finally carry me out of a world of infinitely unmeetable expectation, the world of the old creation, and into the life of the resurrection.

This did not happen, however, without the creation first of further internal obstacles. Although I intended to study the language of Hebrew and to avoid the liberal Christianity of the seminary as much as possible, paradoxically, I still had high hopes for that same Christianity. At first, just studying Hebrew seemed to be the way out, but it didn't turn out to be that simple. Years later I would realize that depression is neither a conviction you can choose to abandon, nor a "feeling" or state of mind you can simply decide to ignore, no matter how good your motives. What actually happened in seminary is that my depression grew worse.

By its exaltation of reason, and its suspicion of faith as blind belief, the Unitarian liberalism of the Taylors had offered me a view of the universe that was not based on sin. By its denigration of emotion and its elevation of the "objective," the Taylors' liberalism had suggested to me that I should be able to get rid of my depression just by regarding it as "subjective" and, therefore, unreal. Surely, seminary would give me a way to make this happen.

One of the most important things that attracted me to Protestant liberalism in my seminary years was that it was not the conservative Christianity of my childhood. The liberal Protestantism of the seminary in the early sixties had nothing but contempt for any form of Christianity that was focused on a personal relationship with God, on faith in Jesus' atoning blood shed for individual sins, or heaven and hell. Jesus was not interested in our individual relationships with God. The work of Jesus was to announce the inbreaking of the kingdom of God in this life, as it had been proclaimed by the prophets before him. This was why Jesus had been crucified—because he preached God's radical demand for social justice. In the eyes of my classmates and teachers the most serious issue of social justice that needed to be addressed was racism, and I passionately agreed.

The trouble was that in its own way this form of Protestant liberalism with its emphasis on the cross made me feel more helpless than the conservative Christianity I was trying to escape. As I experienced it in those days, it was a grim religion, and its public and private preaching relied almost entirely on the power of guilt to motivate its listeners—just as much so, in fact, as the revival preachers of my childhood. Now, rather than being warned of the Last Judgment in the light of my metaphysical badness, I heard sermons without limit on Amos: "Why do you seek the day of the Lord? It is darkness and not light. I hate, I despise your feasts. . . ." God was in a rage over the sin of my participation and complicity in the web of racism upon which society was built.

Certainly, I knew that what I heard was right. The racist society of which I was a part by virtue of being white and middle-class really was built on the backs of the poor. My middle-class comforts brought suffering to children, women, and men all over the country I had never even met, and the fact that I had never meant to cause pain did not let me off the hook. Unless I did something about it, I really was contemptible. But what was I to do about it?

The primary answer was "to take up the cross" through social action. "Social action" in my seminary, however, did not mean working in soup kitchens or performing small, private acts of charity or kindness. Social action meant devoting yourself heroically to the radical politics of change, to participation in public demonstrations. Social action meant dropping your concern for the ordinary and small things of the everyday world to sacrifice your life to bring in the Kingdom.

Not everybody was willing to go all the way with social action. What every socially sensitive real Christian could do, however, was to accept that no one had a right to value the ordinary or to be happy in the face of the suffering one caused other people simply by living as part of the middle class. If the Christian did not have the guts to abandon a middle-class life in an overt way, then he or she could still demonstrate solidarity with those who suffered by internally rejecting ordinary life to live in a perpetual state of self-flagellating guilt.

This for me was a deadly message. I had wanted to meet all the conflicting expectations and gain the approval of my family, my husband, and my friends. I had wanted to be good in the eyes of God. Now I wanted the approval of my classmates on the one hand, and all those whom I hurt by my middle-class existence on the other. By being a woman in seminary I was already the object of the hostility and scorn of many of my male classmates and their wives. With my whole heart I was against racism and the suffering it caused. At the same time, not only did I not have the ability or the disposition to do much in politics, I was also a full-time married student in a marriage where the responsibility of shopping, cooking, cleaning, and laundry fell entirely on my shoulders. I was already in trouble at home for forgetting to buy toilet paper, failing to get meals on the table on time, and scorching the shirts when I was studying. Now I was being told that even doing these "feminine" things right was worse than contemptible. (Sexism had not yet been discovered as a social-justice issue in my seminary.) I had no time, no money, and I couldn't drive.

I could not be "socially active" in the only way that was pronounced acceptable by my classmates. I felt I had no choice. Once more I turned against myself to accept this extra burden of guilt. My depression grew.

At the same time, I continued to fight against the depression. Subversively, contradictorily, like a secret vice, I continued to revel in Hebrew and in the glimpses it gave me of another life and another God. Through the promises of Isaiah, the stories of Genesis, the account in the Song of Songs of an ecstatic love that is stronger than death, God was working silently within me.

After two years I left seminary, and I went to graduate school at Oxford University. With great anxiety and great pleasure I completed a first degree in Semitic languages. I began a D.Phil. in Syriac patristics. I marveled over the many women scholars I saw there. In the Bodleian Library I had another epiphany of God through Philoxenus of Mabbug, the heir to the great monastic teachers of the early church, when I learned from him that God's loving and gentle expectations of us are very far from the burdens we lay on one another. In the convent in Oxford I had another epiphany through Mother Jane when I began to learn to trust my own mind. Thus, though the shape and feel of my depression remained, without my realizing it the causes of it were under serious attack.

In actual fact, however, when I returned to the States after three years I soon felt worse than ever. I had come back to the advent of the women's movement, which was enormously helpful, and to the myth of the super-woman, which was not. Now, I tried to be all things to all people in earnest. I tried to please my husband and be a good wife in spite of my vocation as a scholar. I wanted to make my mother proud of me in spite of my absentminded housekeeping and desultory letter-writing. I worked on my dissertation, and I tried to be a good scholar. I gave birth to Anna Grace, and, in spite of the rest of my life, I tried to be a good mother. I began teaching at Notre Dame, and I tried to be a good teacher. I finished my dissertation. I gave birth to Benjamin, and I continued to teach. In spite of how hard I had worked and continued to work, whatever I did, more than ever before, in the eyes of the people who mattered, it seemed to me it was still never enough. I was exhausted, and it is no wonder my depression did not go away.

At the same time, usually in ways I hardly recognized, God was calling me forward into life. I gave up on my marriage, and I was divorced. I moved to Georgia to teach at Candler. I was wonderfully remarried. My research took a different turn as I at last stopped worrying so much about what other, liberal scholars would think about me working on the early monastic writers I had first met in Oxford. I began to pore over these ancient teachers. I learned from them to pray, and both in the good work of ordinary prayer, and in the special, painful work of the extraordinary, I began to know God and I began to know myself as God knows me.

Nevertheless, I was still depressed. Indeed, by the time I was forty-seven years old, my depression finally grew so deep that I might as well have been living in a cave.

The immediate cause was extreme anxiety over my daughter, Grace, though it might just as well have been Benjamin. I had worried over both of them since they were born. Having had such a hard childhood myself, I decided early in life that I never wanted to take the risk of bearing children for whom I might not be able to be a good mother, children whom I might not be able to protect from the kind of childhood unhappiness I had known. The desire to "be good" and meet family expectations, however, had overridden what I felt was my better judgment.

I had been astounded by the reality of both children and the passionate love I felt for them from the time they moved in my body. When they were babies, Grace's bright eyes and Benjamin's calm spirit filled me with holy wonder and joy. I only wanted to hold them, nurse them, watch them sleep. In the extravagant happiness of my love, it seemed to me that, somehow, my own childhood unhappiness would be redeemed.

My anxiety about my motherhood, however, did not go away. As my love grew, so did my desire to be a good mother, both in the eyes of my children and in the eyes of the world. The problem was, what was a good mother? I had the models, of course, of my own mother, both the ways she had been with me as a child, and the ways she was with me as an adult. I had the two ideological models of late sixties and early seventies. I could be an earth-mother who was a "real woman" and nurse my children till they were five years old. Or I could realize that the center of my identity as a woman lay in my career and that it was quality time not quantity of time that made a good mother. Or I could ignore all three of these and just model myself upon the common sense of the expert, Dr. Spock.

And the children were so different from each other! From babyhood Grace had been like me, picking up the emotions of everyone around her, especially mine. Benjamin had been the other extreme, living his own self-contained life from the start. Teaching herself to read at four, Grace had been very verbal, so much so that her second-grade teacher had told me to hide her books. Benjamin, on the other hand, was extremely untalkative. He not only did not learn to read until the second grade; he didn't talk at all until he was over four.

I worried about everything, and my worry didn't let up as they got older. Was I too strict? Was I too lenient? Did I offer them enough opportunities? Did I give them too much to do? Had I talked to Grace enough as a baby? To Benjamin too little? Did I give them enough chores? Too few? Did I put too much pressure on them, supervise their homework enough, intervene enough at school? Did I meddle? Were they happy, and if they were not, should I have been able to make them happy?

It is not surprising that my lifelong depression hit its lowest point on the Friday afternoon before the Saturday night party to celebrate our tenth wedding anniversary. Richard especially, who has an entirely happy disposition and is very good at celebrating, had been looking forward to the party for ten years. Ten years earlier on the afternoon of Easter Sunday, on an earth-smelling, sweet spring day of dogwoods and azaleas and luminous green, we had married.

Our wedding had been a wonderful celebration of Easter. The ceremony in our dining room had been simple. Richard and I had stood in front of the buffet. Four-year-old Benjamin, in shorts and a bow tie, had held Richard's hand. In a grown-up long dress, Grace, who was nine, had stood beside me. Our good friends Bill and Philip, who had driven all the way from South Bend, had taken up their positions to keep new friends and family off the smelly spot in the rug Kitty had made. (He hadn't been able to find the litter for several weeks when we first moved to Atlanta.) My new friends Melissa and Jerome had come in late with an enormous blue striped bowl of strawberries and bananas. Family and other new friends had arranged themselves around the rest of the room. Richard and I had said our vows, and at the end we all sang together an accidentally jazz version of "Joyful, joyful, we adore thee." Then the two of us had stumbled out onto the porch in a haze of the very joy we had sung about.

Ten years later, that Easter of our wedding was still an amazing event to remember, and I wanted for Richard's sake and my own to celebrate it. Yet, here I was, preparing for the celebration with a heart so heavy that it might just as well have been wrapped in wet newspaper. Since Grace had moved the previous summer into a broken-down house in a dangerous part of town, I had worried about her. I had had a frantic call from her that morning. As I struggled with the vacuum cleaner and thought of my inability to keep either of my children safe and happy, I found myself pressed down by the weight not only of my failure as a mother, but of all my failures, of my inability not only to have been the mother I had wanted to be, but the wife, daughter, friend, niece, historian, and teacher I had intended to be as well. The memory of all my unmet obligations, all the people I had hurt, all the suffering I had done, my dirty refrigerator, my unfinished research, my unanswered correspondence hurt my head.

Finally, in a despair new even for me, I dragged myself into my study. I sat down across from my desk in the tall red chair in which I have always had my prayers, and I cried out to God. "I have failed in everything you have given me to do. I have tried so hard to be a good mother. With my whole heart I have wanted to love my children enough to keep them safe and happy. I have suffered with them and for them. I have begged you to help me to love them well and in the right way, but the harder I try the more I worry. There must be something essential about Christianity I am missing, something I can't see. I give up. If there is something you want me to know, you must find me yourself to tell me. I can try no longer, and I can look no longer. I give up. I absolutely give up."

And I did give up, utterly. There in my familiar chair, on that green April afternoon, the light of my life went out. My head fell on my chest and my breathing slowed. My heart was torn in half, and out of those halves ran all the unmet and conflicting expectations, good intentions, and desires to please I had ever had. I didn't care if I was a good mother or a good teacher or a good daughter. I no longer suffered with those who suffered. I did not feel guilty. I did not accept my unhappiness as my due, nor did I reject it. I did not fight against what was happening to me. Emptied, at last, of everything, I finally felt nothing. I simply sank like a dead body into darkness.

How long I sat there in that state, I have no idea. Perhaps it was a long time that passed; perhaps it was simply a moment. I only know that, all of a sudden and without any warning, I woke up. I heard my own voice repeating in my mind the words from the Roman Catholic eucharistic prayers for Easter, "The joy of the Resurrection renews the whole world." Every cell of my body heard them and for the first time I knew that these words were absolutely true, and that they were true for me.

"The joy of the Resurrection renews the whole world," I repeated to myself in wonder, and while I spoke, my long-broken heart was healed. "The joy of the Resurrection," I said to myself, and my heart filled up with a joy so fierce that it spilled out and ran through the whole of my body and flickered around me like a flame. In my red chair I laughed out loud for pleasure, like a drunk or like a little child, and I thought that never, in my whole life, had I ever laughed before. Of course! There was, indeed, something I had missed about Christianity, and now all of a sudden I could see what it was. It was the Resurrection! How could I have been a church historian and a person of prayer who loved God and still not known that the most fundamental Christian reality is not the suffering of the cross but the life it brings? Of course, Jesus did not die to bring death to the world, but to establish the life God intended for us from the beginning. It was so very obvious. The foundation of the universe for which God made us, to which God draws us, and in which God keeps us is not death, but joy.

"The joy of the Resurrection renews the whole world," repeated itself within me, and now I felt or saw, rather than heard, God laugh with joy as God spoke without words within me: "How could you have thought your goodness, your very right to existence depends upon your pleasing even a person so important to you as your own child? Do you not remember that I am the one, the only one, who gives life, the only one who loves you without limit, and I will never withhold it from you?

"And how could you ever have thought that you deserved to suffer, that you should pay for your existence with your suffering, that you could buy off other people's suffering with your own? When you were a child and you made the anger of your parents your own and you turned it against yourself, did it bring you life? When you sank into your mother's grief and bitterness as though it was your own, did it rescue her or help you? When you took upon yourself your daughter's despair, did it lift it off of her?"

There was a pause, and then I heard my own voice repeat once again, "The joy of the Resurrection renews the whole world," and now I saw spread out before me wide fields, summer trees, bright mountains, and human beings without number, those I knew and those I did not, and all were upheld by God's own joyous self, mysteriously, by a love so strong, so supple, and so subtle I could hardly imagine it.

By the light of that love I could see that in my desire to be a good mother, in my lifelong attempts to be found good by the people around me, in my efforts to escape the fact that whatever I did I was always wrong, I had turned in on myself and away from the real world, to live not so much in a cave as in a teacup.

Concerned about my own acceptability, how could I even have seen the people I cared for as separate from myself? How could I have responded to the actual needs of my flesh-and-blood daughter? How could I have let myself know that it is God who holds all living things in existence, not I myself? That it is God who keeps each one of them—my daughter, my son, my mother, my students—in a secret covenant to which I not only have no access but blessedly need no access?

At last I knew fully what I had already begun to learn in my experience of the crucifixion many years before. Truly, Jesus had not died to show me I must earn my right to be loved, nor been crucified so that I would take onto my own shoulders infinite responsibility for the pain of the world. Jesus had died for the New Creation, for the joy of the resurrection of the whole world.

For me that day, the promises of Isaiah had been fulfilled:

> On this mountain the God of hosts will make for
>   all peoples
>   a feast of rich food, a feast of well-aged wines. . . .

And God will destroy on this mountain
   the shroud that is cast over all peoples. . . .
God will wipe away the tears from all faces,
   and the disgrace of God's people God will take
   away from all the earth. . . .
It will be said on that day, "This is our God. . . .
This is God, for whom we have waited;
Let us be glad and rejoice in God's salvation."[1]

On my way to Jerusalem I had at last found that the
Bitter Valley of my life had become a place of springs.[2]
I had sown in tears; I had reaped in joy, and my mouth
was filled with laughter.[3] With my eyes I saw before me
"a new heaven and a new earth; for the first heaven and
the first earth had passed away, . . . and I saw the holy
city, the new Jerusalem, coming down out of heaven
from God like a bride adorned for her husband."[4]

A long time later, as I sat in my chair, the intensity of
my joy and the drunken clarity of my thought subsided.
After a while, I took up my vacuuming, and I dusted. I
cleaned the bathroom, then I threw out some of the
moldy stuff from the refrigerator, and like one miraculously snatched from death, I enjoyed all these everyday
tasks with a single heart. Every fifteen minutes or so for

---

1. Isaiah 25:6-9 (NRSV alt.).
2. Psalm 84:6.
3. Psalm 126:5, 6.
4. Revelation 21:1, 2 (NRSV alt.)

the rest of the weekend, those words repeated themselves to me, burning themselves into my very flesh: "The joy of the Resurrection renews the whole world."

That Easter weekend the God of beauty of my childhood, the God who had come to me in Hebrew and had appeared to me in the cross, lifted me from the grave and brought my forty-five-year depression to an end. Our anniversary party was wonderful. The very air quivered with spring. Richard's hair curled exuberantly. Some of the guests brought a cherry tree in bloom, and a picnic basket and a cookbook. We played loud music, and everyone stood close together and ate and drank and laughed.

Of course in the years that followed all has not always been well. I still struggle, as I should, to push against the terrible injustice of the world, but I do it now from the energizing perspective of joy rather than from the paralyzing perspective of guilt. Though I hardly worry about my housekeeping anymore, I worry about my teaching. I still have periods where I forget to love my children by listening to what they themselves actually need and want, instead of my loving them by being "a good mother," but so what? Even Jesus was resurrected with his wounds.

◊ S I X ◊

Memories of God:
In the Communion
of the Saints

I was not there when my father died in Connecticut on Holy Thursday in 1991, but the death of my Auntie Ree the next year was very different. I had gone off to England to a series of meetings that summer, and she had been away from Atlanta in her wanderings a little over a year. I hadn't heard from her often; she was living with her daughter's family in conditions that made her unable to make or receive phone calls very often. She had called me from the Midwest a few days before I left to tell me that she had had a fall. She wasn't able to get up out of a chair or sit down by herself. They hadn't taken her to a doctor, but her son-in-law, she said, was being terribly nice to her. She wanted me to know about her fall, and I wasn't to worry.

When I returned from England a month later she was in the hospital in Tulsa, and she was dying. I knew this without any doubt because she told me so on the phone every day for two weeks. She was dying; she wanted to die, and she wanted my support. Oh, Auntie Ree!

Ten years earlier I had been living my own life with Anna Grace, Ben, and Richard when my father called one night in April to tell me that one of my cousins, her little daughter, and my cousin's husband would be moving to Atlanta some time soon, and Auntie Ree would be coming along to take care of the baby. I had had almost no contact with her for twenty years. Was I prepared to help her? he wanted to know.

Was I prepared to help her! I had, indeed, not seen her or talked to her in all that time, and I had hardly ever even thought of her. I had never had any adult conversation with her; I didn't count the talk we had had at a fancy New York restaurant the summer I was in seminary. I had been too distracted to remember anything of the visit, except that my aunt's conversation was full of vaguely embarrassing stories of show business people with whom Uncle Vin was working. Through my father over the years I had learned that she wasn't practical in matters relating to my uncle Vin, her children, or money, that she was now almost broke, that she had moved around the country a lot, that her son, my cousin, had died of leukemia, and that she had become a widow. I didn't know much else.

Still, I was ridiculously excited by the prospect of her move to Atlanta. I had never lived in a place that had any family in it since I had graduated from high school, but even more than that, Auntie Ree was special.

One reason for this was that, while I was not much more than a toddler, I had lived for a while with my parents in my grandmother's house in Flushing, New York, and my aunt, a music student at New York University, still living at home, had been there, too. As an adult, I had no distinct or conscious memories of Auntie Ree from that early time, yet paradoxically, I remembered her very well. I had thought her beautiful. She had been tall, with black hair, which she straightened and dark skin like my father, and she had had a round face with a funny way of making her mouth into a circle when she talked or sang to me.

Auntie Ree was the one person in my life who had been for me completely safe. Whatever I did, she thought I was wonderful. In the battle of the beloved Titans over my upbringing taking place in my grandmother's household, she had had no axes either to grind or to wield. She was soft, a person of no substance to the grown-ups in the house, and I had known that they intended for me to see her this way, too. In this they were not entirely successful. I loved her extravagantly in return for her uncritical and affectionate love of me. In my eyes, the grown-ups' dismissal of her only strengthened the secret link between us. Her first name, Marie, and my middle name were even the same.

Not long after my parents and I moved out of my grandmother's house, Auntie Ree married an eccentric and autocratic man who was a writer, first for radio and later for television, and from the beginning of her marriage she danced to his tune. This meant that though she lived fairly close to us a lot of the time while I was a child in New York, I had hardly ever seen her. In spite of her absence, however, in my own mind she and I retained our secret connection. Partly this was because over the years she continued to send me, always late, fabulous gifts for Christmas, wrapped in green or blue or red foil paper, usually with little auxiliary presents hanging from extravagant bows. But partly it was because I believed Auntie Ree alone, of all the grown-ups in my life, both understood me and loved me. My proof was this: when I would irritate my parents by my greedy love of sweets, my messiness, or my desire to talk about things they didn't want me to talk about, they would tell me, "That's enough of that; you are being just like your Auntie Ree!"

When my father called to tell me she was coming to Atlanta, my sense of our mysterious connection was reactivated. I waited for her move with the same painful excitement I awaited a trip to the circus when I was a child. I waited a long time. The chaos of my aunt's life with my cousin's family produced several false starts, and as the months passed, I decided that she was never coming at all. Then, in the February of the next year I had my first call from Auntie Ree herself. They would all be arriving the following Tuesday, and I could call her at the motel on Wednesday.

I hardly slept Tuesday night, and when I did, I dreamed of her vividly as she had been the few times I had seen her as an older child. These dreams were long and complex, and in each of them she brought me elaborately wrapped gifts. In some of the dreams I unwrapped exotic boxes to discover beautiful gold jewelry or shining glass objects whose names I didn't know; in others, the packages were unopened, and anticipated with an anxious wonder.

At five o'clock on Wednesday morning, I gave up trying to sleep and got out of bed. I fixed myself coffee and read some book or other till the paper came, checking the clock every five minutes or so. At seven thirty, I could wait no longer, and I dialed her room. A gravelly voice answered, "Hello?" "Auntie Ree, is that you?" I heard my voice respond, high and tense like a child's. "Yes, my darling, it is," she replied, and my chest heaved, silently. She explained then that having been up all night traveling she had only been in bed an hour. She was eager to see me, but I would have to come in the afternoon.

When at last I pulled my car into the drab but expensive motel in north Atlanta nearly an hour from where we live, my stomach was turning over. I got out, carrying the mottled, hard pralines I had decided to make for her while I waited that morning. My heart racing and my eyes aching with tiredness, I stumbled to her door and knocked. After what seemed a very long time, the door opened. "Auntie Ree?" I asked, shocked at her appearance. "Yes," she said, tentatively. We hugged briefly. I gave her the candy, and we examined each other out of the corners of our eyes as she drew me into the room.

Auntie Ree didn't look at all the way I had anticipated. It was not until that moment, however, that I realized I had expected she would look just the way I remembered her when she had been twenty and I, three. Now, she was an old woman. When I had hugged her she had been stiff and bony. She was still tall, and her clothes were stylish, but her once black hair, though still straightened, was a yellowy silver. Her beautiful olive skin had become a sick grayish yellow that matched her hair, and the cheeks of her round face were hollow, sunken in, and pitted. She walked unsteadily on her high heels with a round-shouldered shuffle that suggested that it was hard for her to keep her balance.

We sat down, she on the bed and I on a nondescript muddy brown motel chair. Without knowing why, exactly, I was intensely anxious. She chatted about her trip while she opened the plastic bag and took out one of my terrible pralines; then she interrupted herself smiling with delight. "These pralines are wonderful," she said, looking at the piece of candy and turning it over in her hands, "the best ones I ever ate. I can't imagine how you can make candy, just like that, with all the things you have to do!" My anxiety ran out of me like water as her praise filled me to the brim with happiness. Suddenly, she was restored to me just as she had been when I was a child, and I loved this woman still, whom I had known and not known through all my adult life, this woman for whom I suspected all my faults and failures were as insignificant as they had been when I was a child.

It has been long enough now that I hardly remember the end of that first visit. My cousin and her family settled into an apartment in north Atlanta soon after that, and my aunt moved close by them into a large apartment full of the beautiful things she had collected during her marriage to Uncle Vin. I didn't really see her often, though I called her every other day. Auntie Ree had never driven, and my cousin was always busy; so, if we were to visit I went up to where she lived or, what she liked best, I brought her back with me so that I could cook her a fancy meal and she could visit Grace and

Benjamin and Richard, whom she was convinced were the smartest, most talented, and lovable teen-aged girl, boy, and man in the world. She began at once to spend most of her holidays with us. She gave us all extravagant gifts simply by the way she so thrived on our attention and love.

She quickly needed a lot. Soon after we first saw her, all of us realized that she was not old—after all, she was only sixty-four when she first came to Georgia—she was desperately ill. The slightest exertion would put her out of breath, and walking a hundred feet very slowly would exhaust her. We were all afraid for her. I begged her to go to the doctor, but she knew the doctor would discover something serious, and she insisted she couldn't afford to know about it until she turned sixty-five and Medicare would pay her bills.

During November of her first year in Atlanta her health suddenly got much worse, and I was terrified that she would die before Christmas. Over her protests, in early January I got her to a doctor who pronounced her in need of immediate heart surgery. My cousin and her husband insisted she have the surgery at a clinic in Houston and flew her to Texas. My aunt returned two weeks later with a new valve on one side of her heart and nothing working at all on the other. She was alive, but terribly weak and mentally confused by the wrong dose of medication the hospital had sent her home with.

In the months that followed I cared for her as best I could, considering how far away she lived. I made her gallons of chicken soup, which was all she wanted to eat for weeks, and I talked with her endlessly, on the phone and in person when I delivered the soup. Mostly, I just cherished her and the love she shone on me.

Whatever good I did her, I thrived myself on my physical and emotional care for her. Abba James, one of the ancient Egyptian monastic teachers who have been so helpful to me over the years, used to say, "It is better to receive hospitality than to offer it,"[1] and in the time I spent with Auntie Ree I discovered what that surprising saying from the desert really meant.

Both of my parents had valued the virtues of strength and self-sufficiency as long as I could remember. When I was a child my father, in his manly way, had seemed in need of nothing, especially from me. During most of my life my mother had always been a generous giver and helper of others including me, but she could not receive anything herself without feeling "beholden." It had seemed to me that I could never find a way to give anything meaningful to her that she could really accept, either in the way of gifts or help. Even my generous husband, who had no trouble with being "beholden," would not let me give him gifts.

---

1. James, 1, *The Sayings of the Desert Fathers,* trans. Benedicta Ward, S.L.G. (London and Oxford: Mowbray, 1981), p. 104.

It is hard to explain to a loving person who can only give, what this refusal to receive does to the would-be givers. If our gifts come out of the substance of who we are, to refuse our gifts is a rejection of our very self. At the same time, the turning away of a gift destroys the reciprocity of love. In place of mutuality, it sets up a hierarchy of love that makes the one who always receives and whose gifts are refused feel empty, powerless, and incompetent to love well, and so unable in turn to receive from the beloved with a grateful heart.

Perhaps this is why certain theological approaches to God want to insist that God needs nothing from us, that God is the only one who can give, while everything we have to give already belongs to God anyway. To think of God as above being able to receive our gifts keeps us aware at all times that our relationship with God isn't really based in the mutuality of love so much as it is based in God's unspeakable power and glory, and our deplorable weakness and sin.

This is not, however, the baby Jesus, who receives gifts of gold, frankincense and myrrh, or the adult Jesus, either, who receives the gift of perfume from a woman who pours it over his feet, as well as the friendship and consolation of Martha and Mary. In the Old Testament, too, God is offered and gladly receives sacrifices, of heifers, wheat, and praise by those who love God, and the hearts of God's lovers are strengthened and gladdened in return.

I don't know if my aunt could have articulated any of this. Abba Poemen said "that Abba John said 'that the saints are like a group of trees, each bearing a different fruit.' "[2] I know that the fruit of Auntie Ree's tree was loving, and the juice of that fruit was the way she received as well as gave. She received my hospitality, my help, and my gifts with a happy gratitude, praise, and love. These in turn nourished me and filled me with energy, happiness, and pride, softening my own heart to receive her other gifts.

One of these gifts was conversation. It was wonderful for me to be able to talk to Auntie Ree, this aunt I had supposedly been like as a child. It is reported that Abba Poemen, another of the early Egyptian monastics who have been my friends and guides, was accustomed to tell his disciples, "Teach your mouth to say that which you have in your heart"[3]; and now I began to learn the value of this saying, too. It was not merely an admonition to honesty. It was a firm conviction of the desert teachers that the negative power of our "unspeakable" secret memories, self-judgments, temptations, and passions comes precisely from their being unspoken and un-shared. What those who would live in the way of love had to learn to do was to speak the truth to their teachers or to their companions.

---

2. Poemen 43, in *The Sayings of the Desert Fathers,* p. 95.
3. Poemen 63, in ibid., p. 175.

This was my need, too. I grew up in a family in which only the positive could be spoken. In spite of good friends in the present and a husband who loved me with his whole heart, I had lived lonely my whole life, in the hidden power of my own unspeakable questions and musings, my grief and anger, frustration and sadness, confusion and envy. Because of the power and content of this inner, unspeakable me and its difference from my acceptable public self, even as a child I had been guiltily aware of myself as somehow double, and so cut off from those around me. I had already begun to learn the freeing power of speaking my heart to God. Now, I began to experience what it meant to me to be able to "speak with my mouth what I had in my heart" to this woman of my own family who knew me and loved me, and whom I had loved for so long.

There was nothing I could not say to her. All the things that I could not talk about in my growing-up years and my adult years, too, I spoke to her. I spoke of my own upbringing, of my forbidden childhood sadness, of my failures and humiliations as a schoolchild and as a daughter, of my fear of my father, of my shame over being female, of my grief following my parents' divorce, of my long first marriage with its own grief and terrible anger, of my lifelong depression. I talked, too, about my happy second marriage, my prayer, my teaching, my theological reflection, and my children. Auntie Ree listened to all of it with love and without passing judgment, and I think she understood nearly everything she heard. The winding cloths of Lazarus began to loosen around me.

At the same time, my father's sister held back nothing of herself or her own life. She told me story upon story not only of her up-and-down marriage and the hard time she had had since she had become a widow. She spoke to me of the life she and my father had had growing up with my grandparents in Manhattan. I heard for the first time of my grandmother's argumentative harshness to the little children my aunt and father had been, and of my grandfather's ongoing cruelty to them both. I learned from her, too, of my poor grandmother's own childhood suffering at the hands of her aristocratic German immigrant mother. She told me what she knew, as well, of the childhood of her father, whose father died before he was born, the only child of an immigrant widow left without a penny.

What a gift all these family stories, and particularly my father's story were! It had been a long time since my own heart had been touched when I had first encountered the teaching on judgmentalism of the early monastics in Philoxenus of Mabbug's *Thirteen Ascetical Homilies*. I had pondered for years their insistence that only the compassionate God can judge us because only God has complete knowledge of the depth of our struggles, of our temptations and our sufferings that come before our sins. In the telling of those stories my aunt

gave to me, I believe, lay some part of God's own
compassionate knowledge of my father and my grandmother. My heart began to heal as my pain and anger
toward my father was replaced with the gift of yearning
love toward the harassed little boy my father had been.
It was at this time that I made my first adult visit to my
father at Auntie Ree's urging, and at the urging of my
early monastic teachers who insisted that it was not
enough that I simply forgive my father in my heart.
What a miracle of blessing for us both were those years
of love and friendship between my father and me before
his death!

At last my aunt began to recover from the surgery.
After more than a year, Auntie Ree still walked with a
shuffle and she had no stamina at all, but her color was
back. She was as well as she ever was going to get. She
had two or three more years of real happiness. Then
began the long series of moves that preceded her accident the summer she died. First, her daughter's family
went to Monaco and afterwards to Florida, and during
that time my aunt moved closer to us. We continued our
talks. I took her shopping once a week and tried to take
her on little outings. She saw the children frequently. She
often came to our house for dinner. I loved to cook for
her the foods she loved to eat, roast chicken and mashed
potatoes, lasagna, exotic Italian dishes, and above all,
fruit pies of all sorts, and yellow cakes with fudge icing.
I can still see her in our kitchen, sitting on the high stool

in her fancy silk dresses as I would cover my hands and clothes with flour, constructing for her a last-minute cherry pie. "Nobody can cook like you can, my darling," she would say, shaking her head in wonder over my good but perfectly ordinary pie. Those were happy years for us together, and I think we both expected they would last forever.

This was not to be the case. When I returned from England during the summer of my aunt's second year on our side of town, everything had changed. My cousin had come back, broke, from Florida, to move into my aunt's tiny apartment with her own little girl and box upon box of their possessions. Now my aunt let her life be set entirely by theirs. My cousin and her daughter went to bed late every night and slept past noon every afternoon. Auntie Ree preferred not to disturb them by talking on the phone while they slept, and when they were awake, my cousin used the phone. The only time I talked to my aunt was when they went out. They didn't go out often, and she didn't want to go out without them, so Auntie Ree rarely left home herself.

It was a hard time for me. After losing her as a child and then having her as an adult, I had lost her again, and I was left dull and bewildered by my loss. After a year or so, my cousin's husband finally returned from his own wanderings. It was only a small further blow when they rented a house even farther from us than their original Atlanta apartments, and Auntie Ree, really broke now, moved into a single room in a retirement home close to them.

Within a few months her daughter's family moved again to California, and my aunt was left in the retirement home on the other side of town. I was lucky to see her once a month. From the time her daughter had originally moved in with her we had lost our habit of talking nearly every day on the phone. I had made myself very busy with my family, my teaching, my friends, and my writing. I loved her as much as ever, and I knew she loved me in the same way, but from my side, something was damaged between us. I think it was my grief that made me craven about allowing myself to get so close to her again—my grief that followed upon the sure knowledge that it was only a matter of time until she went away for good.

The time was not far off. Auntie Ree was never a particularly gregarious person, and though she didn't complain, I knew she was bored and lonely by herself in the retirement home. Within a year or two when my cousin invited my aunt out to California to live with them, she accepted. That May, in the midst of giving finals and grading them, I drove almost every day for a week or two to Roswell to do her heavy packing. The task was as exhausting as all tasks are when their end result is loss. I wrapped each picture in big sheets of newsprint, each bowl and each lamp, knowing that I was seeing it for the last time.

The day she left we both cried inconsolably. "You are like my own daughter," she said to me again and again through her tears. "How can I bear never to see you again?" "I'll visit you in California," I cried in return, but we knew that this would never happen.

I hardly ever heard from her after she left. I knew it was not through lack of love. Like me she had an almost pathological inability to write letters, and she did not like to call me when the family was there. My cousin's husband worked at home and never wanted the phone tied up. For a year or more, when my cousin and her husband were out, Auntie Ree would phone me to ask how we were and to tell me about my cousin's photography and her granddaughter's successes in school. I found it painful to talk to her. She wasn't feeling well, and no one had time to locate the doctors she needed or take her to them. I knew she didn't want to go herself, and so she wouldn't insist. She was taking a big risk; the medicines she was on for her damaged heart were strong and easily out of balance.

It was during Holy Week of that first year in California that my father died, and that fall came my mother's heart surgery from which she almost died, too. The next January my cousin's family and my aunt were on the move again, in preparation for a business move to the Isle of Man. This time they were truly on the road, traveling in two cars by a circuitous route through the Southwest to my cousin's husband's family home in

Oklahoma. They were on the road for months. I rarely knew where any of them were, but I would get a desperate phone call from Auntie Ree every few weeks. Auntie Ree was worn out. It was clear she was not going to make it to the Isle of Man. When she called after her fall in Oklahoma I knew she was at the end of the line, and I went off to England determined not to think about her or feel anything until I got back.

I am not sure what I expected to find at the end of the month I was away, but I wasn't prepared for what I found. Auntie Ree was in the hospital in excruciating pain with a broken hip and a four-inch gap between the pieces. She was suffering from such serious malnutrition from her hand-to-mouth wanderings that the doctors wouldn't operate to set the break until she ate enough to get stronger. She was beside herself. She knew that her broken hip was not going to heal, and she knew what kind of life awaited her when she left the hospital. She didn't want the surgery. She didn't want to live, and so she refused to eat. She wanted me to support her in her desire to die. The hospital was desperate, too. They were not interested in what might happen to her later; they only wanted her alive, now. Against her wishes they were dripping glucose, vitamins, and antibiotics into her arms, and they had given her at least one blood transfusion over her protests.

I needed to go to Tulsa but I couldn't go until we took Benjamin off to Indiana for his first semester at college.

In the meanwhile, Auntie Ree and I talked every day by phone. Most of the time she seemed to be perfectly herself. She didn't seem depressed. She complained of the painful treatments and the doctors who wouldn't listen to her, and she praised the care and gentleness of the nurses. She worried about her appearance and was pathetically pleased, considering her malnutrition, that she weighed less than she had in years. She talked about her grandchild. She wanted to hear everything about Benjamin's preparations for college, as well as what the rest of us were doing.

She also, however, never let me forget her intention to die and the moral support she wanted from me while she accomplished it. She knew the surgery was coming soon, and she did not wish or expect to survive it. She told me repeatedly that she needed me there with her in spirit, and that, in order to be with her, I would have to let her go. She knew how hard for me what she asked of me was, and she tried as best she could to make it easier. To prepare me for what was coming, she went over all our good times together and she told me what she wanted me to remember in the future. She repeated to me over and over how much she loved me and how she would always be with me.

Two days before we left Benjamin at college, Auntie Ree and I said good-bye for what we believed would be the last time. The next day they began the surgery to set her hip. They found it so full of infection, however, that they decided they couldn't set the bone until the infection healed, so they simply sewed her back up and began to give her even more massive doses of antibiotics. She was half out of her mind when I talked to her next, in terrible pain as well as despair. They not only wouldn't let her die; they intended to operate again.

Without telling her I was coming, the day after we returned from taking Benjamin I flew out to Tulsa. When at noon I walked into her room in the hospital I found her with her eyes shut and her shoulders bare, propped up a little in a high, barred bed facing the shaded window. Against the wall behind her stood a tall bank of blinking machines. From both of her blue-veined hands stretched clear tubes leading to upside-down bottles hanging on little stands above her head. It was shocking to me that, in spite of everything, she looked exactly the way I had seen her last.

I stood beside her bed a moment, full of love and grief. Then I called her name. "Auntie Ree?"

Her eyes opened and she looked around. Then, her face filled with joy. "Is it you my darling?" she said. "Is it really you?"

"It is really me," I answered, my own face full, I am sure, of an answering love and joy.

All afternoon we both existed in a kind of exaltation of love. She held my hand while we talked. She told me again the story of her life, of her losses and her happinesses, of what I had meant to her. She showed me a picture of her granddaughter, and I showed her pictures of Anna Grace and Benjamin and Richard. She introduced me to the nurses. She told me again of the help she needed from me, and of her concern that I would blame myself once she was dead. Toward the end of the afternoon I played part of a Bach sonata for her on my flute.

The evening continued quiet. The doctor came in in his white coat about eight. My aunt made him promise there would be no more blood transfusions, then he and I went out to the hall to talk. I explained to him that my aunt really did want to die, that she wanted no more medical intervention, and certainly not another operation.

"I'm sorry, but I can't let her make that decision," he had replied.

"Why not?" I asked.

"Because she is not in her right mind," he answered.

I stared at him. "How can you say that?" I wanted to know. "She is exactly the same in her mind as she has always been."

"She's depressed," he said.

"What makes you say that?" I wanted to know.

"She wants to die," he said. "That proves it."

"But that is a circular argument," I cried. "You are saying that anybody who wants to die is automatically crazy! She knows very well what her life will be. Have you asked her about that?"

"We have an ethics board, professional theologians who know a lot more than you do, and this is what they have decided," he answered.

"I am a professional theologian, and I am married to an ethicist. I am perfectly capable of making my own decisions," I said, enraged. "What are her chances of living even crippled if you operate again? Ten percent?"

He paused a long time. "Not as much as that," he said before he left.

I returned to the room, and my aunt and I continued to chat. At one point she asked me to pray for her. In this, I failed her. With a constricted throat, I could not pray loud enough for her to hear me the first time, and she asked me to pray again, louder. I imagined, even then, that I still couldn't make myself heard for her. At ten-thirty Auntie Ree began to doze. With sheets and blankets the nurses brought I made up a bed on the couch in her room and tried myself to settle in to rest.

Then, at eleven o'clock a blond woman in stretch pants entered the room with an enamel cart full of test tubes and needles.

"Who are you?" I asked, sitting up out of a light sleep.

"I'm here to get her ready for her blood transfusion," she answered, jerking her head toward my aunt.

"The doctor told me I didn't have to have any more," my aunt replied, firmly.

"I'm sorry," she said, shrugging. "I'm only the technician." She went on, drawing blood from one of the tubes in the back of my aunt's hand. "He told me himself that you have to have a transfusion tonight."

I called the nurse, who came immediately. "I won't let them give you blood if you don't want it," she said to my aunt. "I'll call the doctor."

By this time it was nearly midnight. The nurse was gone a long time, and when she returned her mouth was set in a firm line. "He insists that she have the blood," she said to me. "I'm calling the nursing supervisor. It may be a while before I talk to her, so you go on back to bed."

Profoundly anxious, I lay back down and closed my eyes. I must have slept because the next thing I knew the sheering light of the overhead fluorescent bulbs was blinding me. The room was full of people and equipment. I leaped to my feet completely awake, my heart pounding. The nursing supervisor was on top of me in a flash. The clock on the wall read two o'clock.

"Why are you interfering in this way?" she demanded to know. "You are killing your aunt. Don't you even care? How can you treat her like this if you love her? Don't you care about the position you are putting us in in the hospital?" She looked at me, frowning.

I explained again that my aunt was perfectly capable of making her own decision, and because I did love her I had to support her in it, whatever my own personal desires for her might be. I was sorry about the hospital, but I owed it nothing. My loyalty was to my aunt.

Then she turned away and walked to where Auntie Ree lay, following everything. I placed myself on the other side of my aunt's bed and took her hand. The nursing supervisor glared down at her. My aunt was not in the least intimidated. "If you give me that blood transfusion I'll sue the hospital," my aunt glared back.

The supervisor pleaded some more. Finally, they all left without giving her the blood. At six o'clock just as it was beginning to get light the doctor arrived. "Well, you've won," he told us. "We're stopping everything but the morphine."

When he left, my aunt's happiness was overflowing. "You have given me eternity, my darling," she said to me, and she thanked me again and again for helping her fight for herself. Soon, a nurse came in, turned off all the machines, and took out of my aunt's body every tube but one. She hooked up the morphine and showed my aunt how to push the button when she needed it. Then we were alone. I held Auntie Ree's hand as she fell asleep.

I stood there, looking at her dear face two more hours. Though I called her name and shook her a little before I finally left, Auntie Ree never heard me.

After I got home that night I called her; she was already a little confused. She could listen to me, but barely whisper, herself. She was happy that her daughter was there. My cousin called me the next afternoon in Atlanta, sobbing, to tell me that she had stayed with her mother through the night, and that my aunt had only just died, holding her hand.

As for me, I was in shock. A few days after she was gone, I dreamed that I had been out in the car, and as I turned the corner to return home, our house was on fire. I pulled the car over to the curb and watched for a moment as rubber-suited firemen tried to fight the fire in vain. In a moment or two, while I looked helplessly on, my house burnt until nothing was left of it, and the ground was strewn with ashes. In a few more minutes grass grew up where the house had been, so that there was no sign that anyone had lived there at all.

It is only now, more than a year after her death, that memories of Auntie Ree have begun to come back to me. It is only now that my shock has abated. In its place I find my tears flowing out of me in great waves which carry on their crests images as luminous and compelling as dreams. I see my aunt sitting across from me in the Italian restaurant in which we went to eat the last week she was in Atlanta. I watch her hands doing the needle-work she so enjoyed. She is at the dinner table of our house, laughing at Richard's jokes; in my kitchen; lying in bed waiting for me to bring her chicken soup; looking at the Christmas tree. She is riding in my car, and she is calling me "my darling," telling me she will always be with me. I grieve and I am filled with a humble gratitude for her mysterious, healing coming into and going out of my life.

Who was my aunt? She was a perfectly ordinary woman in most respects, about whom to the impartial eye there was nothing special, no great accomplishments or talents a stranger might admire. She lacked common sense in a big way when it came to money. Not a particularly religious woman, with her whole heart she did believe in the love of God and the continuation of our life in God's presence after death. I knew her to be remarkably brave and adventurous, and that she had unusual skills at contentment. Most of all, what I met in her was a genius for loving and eliciting love in return.

She was also a saint. She was a saint in that she loved and was beloved of God, as God loves and cherishes and knows each of us so well that even the hairs of our heads are numbered. In a special way, however, she was a saint because her loving was so like God's.

* *

Dorotheos of Gaza, a sixth-century teacher, once preached a sermon for the monks in his monastery who were grumbling that they were unable to love God properly because they had to put up with one another's ordinary, irritating presence. No, Dorotheos told them, they were wrong. He asked them to visualize the world as a great circle whose center is God, and upon whose circumference lie human lives. "Imagine now," he asked them, "that there are straight lines connecting from the outside of the circle all human lives to God at the center. Can't you see that there is no way to move toward God without drawing closer to other people, and no way to approach other people without coming near to God?"[4]

There is something implied in the very shape of his imagined chart, however, that Dorotheos did not draw to the attention of his listeners—that in the movement toward love, whether of God, or of another human being, there is an open space so close to the center of reality, that the human and the divine loves become indistinguishable. This, I believe, is the place of the Incarnation into which are gathered all the saints like my aunt, like Philoxenus, like Dorotheos, like Julian of Norwich and Mother Jane, who make up the body of

---

4. *Dorotheos of Gaza: Discourses and Sayings,* trans. Eric P. Wheeler (Kalamazoo: Cistercian Publications, 1977), pp. 138-39 (paraphrase).

Christ, and into this place we are all drawn by love, both human and God's. In this place the fixed boundaries of time are overcome. There we may converse with and be blessed by the saints. There we are taught and blessed by the dead as easily as by the living, and our wounds are healed as we traverse what once seemed to be the fixed boundaries even of our past.

The place of the saints, the center of the circle, is not "nowhere"; it is a place in time on this earth, of mountains and valleys, lakes and deserts, bright stars and clouds, in which we must work and suffer, love and be silly, die and be mourned in the everyday, consecutive ways of time. Though love is its foundation, death and loss and grief hold terrible power here, power of such a force to make even Jesus weep. And yet this place is also the heavenly city, God's eternal present, a many-mansioned dwelling in the heart of God.

In October of 1993 I was invited to Ashland, Kentucky, to be a speaker for the annual conference of the Kentucky Council of Churches. I was looking forward to going, but they needed me for a Thursday night, and I had to be back by 12:30 Friday for my afternoon seminar, so it had to be a fast trip. I left class a little early Thursday morning to go to the airport.

On the whole, leaving for Ashland was easy. Not really being a morning person, however, coming home was not so simple. I hated getting up at 5:00 A.M. to catch a ride to the airport with the energetic Disciples of Christ minister who was my host. The car ride was hard. On the way to the airport the only thing contrasting with the midnight blackness of the morning was the patches of fog so thick and white that our headlights hardly penetrated them. I was glad at last at 6:15 to stagger to the right front seat by the window of the little plane.

Once in the air, things were better. Within a few minutes we were above the fog and flying over the mountains. I sunk into my seat and looked across the aisle to watch the sun rise in the east in a horizontal line of intense red over the tops of the mountains. The coming up of the sun was incredibly beautiful. In its early morning splendor the sun was indeed "like a bridegroom coming forth from his tent."[5] For a long time I looked through that eastern facing window before it occurred to me to turn my head to see what I could see to the west through the window immediately beside me.

When I looked out the west window I was amazed. Where I had been gazing before into morning sky, now I was looking down into mountains barely touched by dawn. I looked ahead and saw that we were about to fly over an enormous, island-studded lake that lay forking and gleaming through the valleys of the mountains. The lake seemed supernaturally beautiful as it shone against the spiky darkness of the mountains that

---

5. Psalm 19:5.

rose for miles above its banks. "Where am I?" I asked myself in amazement. "What is this lake before me?"

In search of some familiar landmark I raised my eyes to the western horizon. All of a sudden I realized that I was looking at the twinkling lights of a vast and beautiful city that extended across the whole field of my vision beyond the mountains themselves and the lake below me. "Where are we?" I asked myself, again. "What could this enormous city be, so wide and so brightly lit this early in the morning?" And then, all at once, my heart rose to my throat with joy, for it seemed to me that it was the New Jerusalem[6] I saw, the dwelling place of the saints, the City Set on a Hill, whose maker and builder is God.

I stared and stared at that bright city as I wondered over its inhabitants. Then, glancing down again to try once more to orient myself, I saw that though we were still flying over the mountains, the lake was gone. In its place I was only looking down through the broken places in the mist and fog, down through what I had taken to be a lake with islands, to the bottoms of the deep valleys. I raised my eyes to the city, the New Jerusalem. It, too, was gone, and what I saw now in place of that city, hanging above the mountains on the western horizon, was only a narrow cream-colored

6. Revelation 21.

bank of clouds, touched by the brightness of the sun, rising in the east.

There grew within me a deep thankfulness for this glimpse of the heavenly city of the saints. It is here among us at this very moment, mostly invisible. If we watch for it, and our hearts are truly open to it, then sometimes we are given glimpses of the cloud of witnesses, our beloved as well as our unknown dead, among whom the Letter to the Hebrews tells us we live.[7] Sometimes we come upon the footprints "where bright angel feet have trod," and sometimes, in especially blessed moments, if we listen carefully to their stories, if we watch them go about their days, we see our own sisters and brothers, aunts and uncles, teachers and strangers, clothed like the mountains with glory, held in life forever in the memories of God.

---

7. Hebrews 12:1.